Good with Words

writing and editing

Patrick Barry

Feedback from students at the University of Michigan Law School who took the class version of *Good with Words: Writing and Editing*

"Hands down best class I have taken in the law school. Probably should be a required first-year class. I know that if I took this class my 1L year instead of my 3L year I would have been a better student and a stronger intern."

"I tell everyone I talk to that they should take this class. It has been a gift to have time set aside to learn about the art and science of writing."

"I looked forward to his class every week—and that's saying something for a class that meets on a Friday afternoon."

"This course should be required, either at the 1L or 2L level. It was perhaps the most important course I took at the law school. Learning about the mechanics of writing is something that is forgotten yet so important for us as future lawyers."

"One of the BEST courses I've ever had in law school."

"Professor Barry is a phenomenal teacher. He cares about his students and teaches in a way that is memorable and effective!"

"I loved the class and highly recommended it to my friends."

"Professor Barry created an interesting, informative, and helpful course. I enjoyed his assignments because they forced me to read non-legal work and familiarize myself with good writing—something I do not do while in law school."

"This was a great course, and Professor Barry got everyone involved and excited about being better writers. It went beyond writing a better brief and touched on things that I never realized I could improve."

"I cannot thank Professor Barry enough for the amount of time and work he put into this class. I have benefitted a great deal because of his hard work and will recommend [it] to all students."

"This has been the most helpful class I've taken in law school. I highly recommend every law student take Professor Barry's class. He is great at showing students how to improve their writing one step at a time."

"Patrick Barry is the best professor I've had in law school. He goes out of his way to teach us to write better, but also to become better lawyers and better people. It's obvious that he puts a ton of work outside class into developing the curriculum, and the students are better off for it. I'm incredibly grateful to have taken his class."

"Professor Barry is an excellent teacher. While I can only speak to my own experience, I believe that he did a great job of making the course accessible to every student—a difficult task considering the course is open to 1Ls, 2Ls, and 3Ls."

"Patrick Barry is amongst the best professors I have ever had (if not the best). He cares about teaching. He cares about his students. [And his] class is structured in a way that allows him to truly focus on helping every student achieve their personal best as a writer, putting the focus squarely on growth rather than differentiation. . . . This was easily my favorite class in law school so far."

"Professor Barry is one of the best professors or teachers I have ever had, which is clearly a function of how much he demonstrably cares about pedagogy. The class is always dynamic and interesting."

"Professor Barry goes above and beyond to engage students, empower them, and encourage their pursuits in and out of the classroom."

"I wish that I could have taken more courses with Professor Barry. He was engaging, thoughtful, and dedicated to my success. Being in his class has been a privilege."

Published in the United States of America by
Michigan Publishing

DOI: http://dx.doi.org/10.3998/mpub.9997109

ISBN 978-1-60785-474-6 (paper)
ISBN 978-1-60785-475-3 (e-book)

An imprint of Michigan Publishing, Maize Books serves the publishing needs of the University of Michigan community by making high-quality scholarship widely available in print and online. It represents a new model for authors seeking to share their work within and beyond the academy, offering streamlined selection, production, and distribution processes. Maize Books is intended as a complement to more formal modes of publication in a wide range of disciplinary areas.

http://www.maizebooks.org

For Eva, the best person with whom to spend the most time

I am finishing up my time here at Michigan and am wondering if you have a book. I want to refer to your lectures in the future.

—email from third-year law student at the University of Michigan, June 2016

*How persuasive can you expect to be
if you are not good with words?*

—written on the board in class, April 2017

CONTENTS

CONTENTS

CONTENTS

ONE

The Words
Under the Words

*People don't choose between things, they
choose between descriptions of things.*

—Daniel Kahneman, winner of the
2002 Nobel Prize in Economics

The Words Under the Words: Concept

I don't think writers are sacred, but words are. They deserve respect. If you get the right ones in the right order, you might nudge the world a little.

—Tom Stoppard, *The Real Thing* (1982)

The lawyer looked surprised. "Okay, then," he said, and got up a little too hastily, as though grateful that his job had been made easier. Obinze watched him leave. He was going to tick on a form that his client was willing to be removed. "Removed." That word made Obinze feel inanimate. A thing to be removed. A thing without breath or mind. A thing.

—Chimamanda Ngozi Adichie, *Americanah* (2013)

The words you choose can change the decisions people make. Psychologists call the mechanics of this choice "framing." They've found, for example, that more people will decide to have a surgery if they are told that the "survival rate is 90%" than if they are told that the "mortality rate is 10%." They've also found that having to pay a "surcharge" for using a credit card rankles people more than if they were simply told they would get a "discount" for using cash. They've even found that people enjoy meat labeled "75% lean" more than they do the same meat labeled "25% fat." Framing, it seems, extends all the way to taste buds.

The researcher who pioneered the study of framing in the courtroom is the psychologist Elizabeth Loftus, whose expertise has been used in trials as different and influential as those of O. J. Simpson, Timothy McVeigh, and mass murderer Ted Bundy. One of Loftus's most well-known experiments showed that changing just a single word when questioning eyewitnesses about a car accident can significantly alter their memories of that accident. If you ask witnesses, "Did you see the broken headlight?" you'll likely get more witnesses to say yes than you would if you instead ask them, "Did you see a broken headlight?"

This discrepancy persists even in scenarios where none of the cars in the accident actually had a broken headlight. Simply asking the question using the definite article "the" instead of the indefinite article "a" seems to create a (false) broken headlight in people's brains.

Keep these findings in mind when you approach any piece of writing. Think about more than just the straightforward definition of the words you use. Think about the connotations of those words as well—the ideas they might evoke, the reactions they might elicit, the images and emotions they could stir up.

The poet Naomi Shihab Nye has a wonderful phrase for all this below-the-surface content. She calls it, in a poem about her grandmother, "the words under the words."

The next time you write an email, tell a story, or send someone a text, think about the words under the words in the message you hope to communicate. The same goes for any official document you are asked to put together. It could be a contract. It could be a mission statement. It could be a grant or essay or pitch deck. Whatever you are asked to compose or whatever you decide to compose on your own, the words under your words will play a role. Be aware of the work they are doing.

"Password"

Being aware of the words under your words is especially important when crafting headings. From legal briefs to personal blogs to office memos, headings represent some of the most valuable written real estate around. They give you a chance to frame an issue and plant ideas even before the reader gets to the main text. Treat them like headlines in a newspaper. That level of economy, that level of precision, is required—as is the understanding that a busy reader might not read much else.

Take, for example, a heading from an appeal handled by the University of Michigan Law School's Unemployment Insurance Clinic, which is a group of faculty and students who give free legal representation to aggrieved workers. The case involved a client, Mr. Louis,* who had worked as a pharmacist for more than a decade in a busy Detroit hospital. We don't need to go into all the details of the case; it is enough to know that during a particularly hectic day, Mr. Louis used the computer password of a coworker so he could more quickly fill prescriptions for patients waiting in line. Using somebody else's password was (unbeknown to Mr. Louis) against company policy. So Mr. Louis was fired.

The law students who represented Mr. Louis did not appeal the pharmacy's decision to fire him. His termination was perfectly legal. What they appealed was whether his actions that day rose to the level of misconduct necessary to keep him from getting unemployment benefits. Here is the heading they used to argue that his actions did not indeed rise that high. It could use some editing.

> Given that Mr. Louis maintained a good-faith belief that he could more rapidly serve patients by utilizing a pharmacist's password, he was not willfully and wantonly disregarding his employer's interest and thus should not be disqualified from unemployment benefits.

One reason this heading could use some editing is because the whole thing is too long and unwieldy. It's tough even to think about the words under the words when there is so much other junk in the way.

Another reason involves the phrase "utilizing a pharmacist's password." Put aside for the moment how "utilize" may strike many readers as an ugly, pretentious substitute for "use."** Focus instead on the

---

* The client's name and some other small details about the case have been changed for privacy purposes. Similar precautions have been taken throughout the book.

** Readers of *The Elements of Style* by William Strunk Jr. & E. B. White may remember the authors asking this condemnatory question: "Why say 'utilize' when there is the simple, unpretentious word *use*?" William Strunk Jr. & E. B. White, THE ELEMENTS OF STYLE 50 (4th ed., Boston: 1999).

last two words: "pharmacist's password." Those words pose a bit of a problem for Mr. Louis—which means they also offer an opportunity: some careful editing could make a major impact.

The students representing Mr. Louis were fortunate because there is case law in Michigan that says if you are fired for actions you thought were actually helping your employer, you are not necessarily disqualified from receiving unemployment benefits. But the help this case law gives to Mr. Louis might get lost if the reviewing judges fixate on the word "password," a term that, especially when paired with a verb that says Mr. Louis took something from somebody else, doesn't put Mr. Louis in the best light. The words under the words of "password" connote an invasion of privacy. They suggest, in this context, shiftiness—even theft.

The students could address these concerns by ditching the term "password" and reframing the whole heading to better show that (1) Mr. Louis was simply trying to help the pharmacy serve its clients and (2) Mr. Louis's actions therefore do not rise to the level of misconduct required to disqualify him from unemployment benefits. Here is the original heading again:

> Given that Mr. Louis maintained a good-faith belief that he could more rapidly serve patients by utilizing a pharmacist's password, he was not willfully and wantonly disregarding his employer's interest and thus should not be disqualified from unemployment benefits.

And here is a new version, after several rounds of editing:

> Mr. Louis's good-faith effort to help the pharmacy more quickly serve its patients does not rise to the level of misconduct required to disqualify him from unemployment benefits.

Notice the use of "good-faith effort" right at the beginning of the heading. Similar words appeared in the students' draft as well, but now they are quickly followed by the phrase "to help the pharmacy." That pairing nicely highlights the point the students need to make to the court: that Mr. Louis wasn't trying to sabotage the pharmacy or in any way shirk his responsibilities. He was just trying to do his job.

Notice also the phrase "rise to the level of." The words under the words of that phrase helpfully indicate that "misconduct" is a high burden. Not just any wrong action will do. As one of the lawyers supervising the students explained during the rewriting phase, "We want to make clear that getting to 'misconduct' involves climbing a big-ass mountain. The judges need to know just how high a bar this is." Inserting "rise to the level of" communicates that information. It plants the big-ass mountain on the page.

Nobody Has a Monopoly on Effective Language

None of these edits will earn anyone a Pulitzer Prize. Nor will they automatically win the case for Mr. Louis. Some might have even made you uneasy. I know my own moral compass starts to twitch when it seems words are being used to manipulate an event or experience, especially when I remember that nobody has a monopoly on effective language. Many glorious deeds have been helped along by powerful phrases, but many terrible deeds have as well. The ability to marshal the words under the words is not reserved for noble minds like Maya Angelou, Nelson Mandela, and Elie Wiesel.

But to be an effective advocate for your clients, for your organization, and for yourself, it is important to embrace the point with which this chapter began: the words you choose can change the decisions people make. Or as the epigraph from Nobel Prize–winning psychologist Daniel Kahneman put it, "People don't choose between things, they choose between descriptions of things."

Knowing that will help protect you from being duped by someone else's words. It will also help you champion the ideas, issues, and causes you think deserve more complete, eloquent articulation. Perhaps the single most important thing advocates of all kinds can do to improve their effectiveness—whether in law, education, politics, business, science, medicine, journalism, or even your own family—is follow this directive: become good with words.

* * *

The chapters in this book are designed to help you do that, as are the Writing Workshops each chapter includes. Treat them all as ways to build your writerly awareness and vocabulary. The goal is not to get every question right or to recognize every reference. The goal is simply to start to pay close attention to the force and flexibility of language, the way words shape everything from custody battles, to sporting events, to how we tell stories about ourselves and others.

A Note About the Writing Workshops

The workshops are all divided into three sections. After reading about a writing concept like "the words under the words," getting the chance to play around with it can be very useful, as can seeing it applied in a wide range of fields. So each workshop has the following three sections:

Questions Section: This section includes multiple-choice questions, matching questions, and open-ended questions. All are incredibly low stakes. You won't be graded on your answers. You won't get points off for guessing wrong or for skipping questions that don't work for you. You'll just be given the chance to stretch your brain a bit and engage in a more active, even playful form of learning.

Examples Section: Some of the examples in this section illustrate the concept; others simply provide another way of articulating it. My hope is that they will all give you a fuller understanding of how to process and ultimately use what you have learned.

Practice Section: Taking directly from the materials I assign when teaching, the exercises in this section offer you the best opportunity to put the lessons of each chapter to work. Ideally, you'll do them with at least one other person. You'll read what they wrote, they'll read what you wrote, and then you'll both exchange feedback. Seeing the choices somebody else makes when writing and editing can be tremendously illuminating. But even if you do the exercises alone or don't do them at all, the Practice Sections are still worth reading. Each contains additional tips and techniques—some on how to use your phone to improve your writing, others on how to free your sentences of "interrupting elements." Perhaps they'll even inspire you to design some exercises of your own. I'd love that.

As for the order of the chapters, I arranged them deliberately. But that doesn't mean I arranged them perfectly. And it certainly doesn't mean that I arranged them perfectly *for you*.

You may decide to skip around. You may decide to read one chapter twice before reading another chapter once. You may decide not to read some of the chapters at all. That's fine with me. All of them are self-contained enough to allow for that kind of customized experience. It's your time you're spending. It's your writing future. Organize it in whatever way you think will be most helpful.

A Note About Me

I have been teaching writing for more than a decade. Sometimes I teach undergraduates. Sometimes I teach professionals. Most often, at least recently, I teach law students at the University of Michigan, where I am a clinical assistant professor of law.

The experience has taught me that although writing is rarely easy, there are ways to make it less hard—and potentially a lot more fun. One of these ways motivates the interdisciplinary nature of this book: connect writing to other areas of interest. When I taught undergraduates—both at the University of Chicago (while I was in law school) and at the University of Michigan (while I went to graduate school)—this often meant using examples from a wide range of possible majors. To connect with humanities students, I used examples from history, literature, art, and philosophy. To connect with science students, I used examples from medicine, engineering, physics, and math.

A similar thing is true now that I teach law students, given that their backgrounds are as various as they are impressive. In one row of my class, there might be a student who studied psychology, a student who studied accounting, and a student who studied biochemistry; in another, there might be a former journalist, an aspiring entrepreneur, and a professional ballerina. Interdisciplinarity isn't just a goal in an environment like that; it's an essential part of each lesson plan.

So is stressing the idea of "deliberate practice," a concept developed by the psychologist K. Anders Ericsson to describe how elite performers develop and maintain their expertise. "The right sort of practice carried over a sufficient period of time leads to improvement," Ericsson explains. "Nothing else."

Ericsson offers this explanation in *Peak: Secrets from the New Science of Expertise*, a book he coauthored with the science writer Robert Pool. In their telling, the "right sort of practice" has several characteristics. Here's one: "It develops skills that other people have already figured out how to do and for which effective training techniques have been established." Here's another: "It requires a person's full attention and conscious actions."

You don't coast through deliberate practice. It is not a passive form of learning and development. In fact, Ericsson and Pool make clear that deliberate practice "takes place outside one's comfort zone and requires a student to constantly try things that are just beyond his or her current abilities." That's not always fun.

But it can be very, very effective.

* * *

I've seen forms of deliberate practice transform the writing abilities of high school students, college students, graduate students, and a wide range of professionals. I've also benefited from it myself in realms outside of writing.

During my senior year of college, I was lucky enough to be named an All-American in men's soccer. It was a very nice honor, particularly given that my school, the University of Chicago, wasn't exactly known for being an athletic powerhouse. (There is a fun—though very likely apocryphal—story about one of the school's influential past presidents summing up his approach to athletics this way: "Every time I feel like doing a bit of exercise, I lie down until that feeling goes away.")

Yet here's the thing: although I ended up an All-American, I started out as a walk-on. I had to earn my spot through an open tryout, weeks after the recruited players had already started training.

There were good reasons for this snub. I wasn't very big. I wasn't very fast. I didn't have a ton of natural talent. The quality that I did have, however, was the quality I now try hard to develop in my students: I was good at getting better. Each year, I listened to my coaches, learned from my teammates, and kept improving game by game, practice by practice. After not playing at all during my first season, I earned a spot on the All-Conference team by the end of my second. Further improvement led to a bump up to the All-Region team by the end of my third season and then that All-America nod by the end of my fourth.

Chicago is a Division III school, so it's not like the next step for me was the MLS, much less Manchester United or Real Madrid. But the experience of gradual, systematic progress taught me a lot about what achievement feels like, how it doesn't happen magically, without effort or setbacks.

In *Champions: The Making of Olympic Swimmers*, the sociologist Daniel Chambliss uses a great term to describe this unmagical process. He calls it "the mundanity of excellence."

Chambliss doesn't mean that excellence is easy or common. He doesn't undervalue the effort and attention elite swimmers devote to training right, eating right, and resting right. Just the opposite, in fact. What distinguishes them, he concludes, are their daily acts of discipline: the time they spend mastering each element of a flip turn, the focus they put on keeping their elbows and head in the proper place every time they take a stroke, the calorie counting they do to make sure they are sufficiently fueled.

Individually, none of these choices is that amazing or difficult. Each is, to return to Chambliss's phrase, rather "mundane." The key is that the swimmers remained committed to making those choices, day after day after day. That's how you become excellent. "Superlative performance is really a confluence of dozens of small skills or activities," Chambliss writes, "each one learned or stumbled upon, which have been carefully drilled into habit and then are fitted together in a synthesized whole. There is nothing extraordinary or superhuman in any of those actions—only the fact that they are done consistently and correctly."

Mary Meagher, one of the gold medalists Chambliss studied, offers a more plainspoken assessment. When asked what people misunderstand most about swimming, she said, "People don't know how ordinary success is."

I think Meagher's observation has wider applications, including to the process of writing. A lot of people unhelpfully romanticize how words become sentences, sentences become paragraphs, and paragraphs become full documents. As Anne Lamott notes in her bestselling book *Bird by Bird: Some Instructions on Writing and Life*, there is this myth that professional writers "sit down at their desks every morning feeling like a million dollars, feeling great about who they are and how much talent they have and what a great story they have to tell; that they take in a few deep breaths, push back their sleeves, roll their necks a few times to get all the cricks out, and dive in, typing fully formed passages as fast as a court reporter."

But that myth, Lamott makes clear, is just "the fantasy of the uninitiated." People who actually write for a living—whether as journalists, novelists, academics, lawyers, you name it—understand that the process involves much more struggle than triumph. "I write one page of masterpiece to ninety-one pages of shit," Ernest Hemingway once told F. Scott Fitzgerald in a letter designed to cheer Fitzgerald's literary spirits. "I try to put the shit in the wastebasket."

Joyce Carol Oates uses similarly vivid terms to describe the pain and tedium often required to complete a first draft, a task she's quite familiar with—she's written more than 40 novels, along with an impressive number of short stories, poems, reviews, essays, and longer works of nonfiction. "Getting the first draft finished," she suggests, "is like pushing a very dirty peanut across the floor with your nose."

And here's a glimpse into the long, fitful approach taken by George Saunders, whose writing has helped him win a National Magazine Award, the Man Booker Prize, and a MacArthur "Genius" Grant, among other honors:

> My method is: I imagine a meter mounted in my forehead, with "P" on this side ("Positive") and "N" on this side ("Negative"). I try to read what I've written uninflectedly, the way a first-time reader might ("without hope and without despair"). Where's the needle? Accept the result without whining. Then edit, so as to move the needle into the "P" zone. Enact a repetitive, obsessive, iterative application of preference: watch the needle, adjust the prose, watch the needle, adjust the prose (rinse, lather, repeat), through (sometimes) hundreds of drafts. Like a cruise ship slowly turning, the story will start to alter course via those thousands of incremental adjustments.

The writer in this model, Saunders explains, is "like the optometrist, always asking: Is it better like this? Or like this?" There is no magical muse. There is no burst of unimprovable eloquence. There is just hard work and craft.

* * *

My students find comfort in descriptions like the ones from Saunders, Oates, and Hemingway. They like learning that even the most expert writers often feel the way they do when faced with a blank page: inadequate, inefficient, only a few seconds away from checking their email instead.

They are also glad to learn that there are concepts and techniques they can use to improve. "The Words Under the Words" is the first of these; the remaining chapters each contain others. When teaching, I usually assign one a week. But you're welcome to go at whatever pace you like or to consider bouncing around unchronologically. You won't run into problems with the sequence of theories or arguments because there is no sequence of theories or arguments. This book is not a work of scholarship.

Instead, it might be better thought of as a work of "teachership"— by which I mean a creative blend of materials developed by a teacher for students, of many varieties and skill levels. There are exercises. There are examples. There are all sorts of ways for you to become a better writer than you are right now.

QUESTIONS SECTION

The doctor was at his midday dinner, which he took at a boardinghouse higher up the main street. When he got back and into his consulting room Tanner asked him what were the life statistics of the North Island.

"Do you mean the death statistics?" the doctor asked.

"They'll do just as well," said Tanner.

—Penelope Fitzgerald, "At Hiruharama" (2000)

The Words Under the Words: Questions*

(1) **Legislation:** The "Death Tax" and the "Estate Tax" refer to the same piece of legislation: a tax on your right to transfer property at your death.

- What are the words under the words of "Death Tax"?
- What are the words under the words of "Estate Tax"?
- Why do you think more people oppose the tax when it is called the "Death Tax" than when it is called the "Estate Tax"?

---

* For answers, see page 219 Appendix C.

(2) **Family Law:** A team of psychologists led by Princeton's Eldar Shafir has found that when people are asked to decide between two parents in a custody dispute, how you frame the question matters a lot. More people will give the child to a parent with a certain set of qualities when the question is "To which parent would you *award* sole custody?" But more will give the child to the other parent—who has a different set of qualities—when the question is "To which parent would you *deny* sole custody?"

Here are the options Shafir and his team gave the decision-makers.

Parent A	Parent B
Average Income	Above-Average Income
Average Health	Very Close Relationship with Child
Average Working Hours	Extremely Active Social Life
Reasonable Rapport with Children	Minor Health Problems
Relatively Stable Social Life	Lots of Work-Related Travel

- How do you think Parent A fared when the question was "To which parent would you *award* sole custody?" Do you think more people picked Parent B? How about when the question was "To which parent would you *deny* sole custody?" Which parent more often got custody then?
- After checking the answers in Appendix C, think about these questions:
  ○ What are the words under the words of "*award* sole custody" that might explain the findings of the study? How about the words under the words of "*deny* sole custody"?
  ○ Which qualities in the parents do you think the decision-makers focused on when they were asked to *award* sole custody to one of the parents? Which qualities do you think they focused on when the question was reframed using the word *deny*?

(3) **Business:** Many companies don't call their workers "employees." Match each company below with the term (or terms) it has used instead.

Company	Term
Trader Joe's	Cast Members/Imagineers
Disney Theme Parks	Baristas
Starbucks	Geniuses/Creatives
Walmart	Food Champions
Apple	Associates
Taco Bell	Crew Members

- What are the words under the words of each of these terms?
- What do the terms signal to customers? What do they signal to managers? What do they signal to other employees?

(4) **Human Trafficking:** Compare these terms for someone who has been trafficked:

a trafficing victim

a trafficking survivor

- How do the words under the words of these terms differ?
- In what contexts might you use one instead of the other?

A similar comparison can be made between a "domestic violence victim" and "a domestic violence survivor," or between a "victim of sexual violence" and a "survivor of sexual violence."

(5) **Education:** In *Work Hard. Be Nice.: How Two Inspired Teachers Created the Most Promising Schools in America*, journalist Jay Mathews notes that the founders of the system of charter schools known as KIPP ("Knowledge Is Power Program") stopped calling the educational excursions they took with their students "field trips." Instead, they started calling them one of the terms below.

(A) field adventures
(B) field works
(C) field lessons
(D) field fun
(E) field free time

After checking the answer in Appendix C, think about these questions:
- What are the words under the words of the right answer? What is being emphasized?
- How might students act during a "field adventure" versus a "field trip"? How about during "field fun" versus "field work"? "Field lessons" versus "field free time"?
- Why might it be easier to get funding from administrators or donors using some of these names rather than using others?
- Which would you pick if you were just trying to get kids excited about going? Which would you pick if you wanted to get kids excited about going but you also wanted to get funding?

EXAMPLES SECTION

For the remainder of the trial, she and her co-counsel, David Paoli, would repeat-
edly refer to Lisak as "the professor from Massachusetts," "the Boston professor," or
some variation thereof, to remind the Montana folk sitting in the jury box that
he was an East Coast intellectual who probably drove a Prius, lived in an ivory
tower, and was out of touch with the real world.

—Jon Krakauer, *Missoula: Rape and the Justice*
System in a College Town (2015)

The Words Under the Words: Examples

(1) **Toni Morrison:** "I wish they would stop calling it welfare and go back to the word they used when my family was a girl. Then it was called, 'Relief.' Sounds much better, like it's just a short-term breather while you get yourself together."

—Toni Morrison, *God Help the Child* (2015)

(2) **Gish Jen:** "What about the years since '73? Had the hotel gotten more dangerous since then, or had other hotels gotten safer?"

—Gish Jen, "Birthmates" (1995)

(3) **Allow vs. Forbid:** "The word 'forbid' seems to be the key to [the difference in people's answers]. Sixty-two percent say 'no' when asked if the United States should <u>allow</u> speeches against democracy, but only 46 percent say 'yes' when asked if such speeches should be <u>forbidden</u>. Evidently the 'forbid' phrasing makes the implied threat to civil liberties more apparent, and fewer people are willing to advocate suppression of anti-democratic speeches when the issue is presented in this way."

—Donald Rugg, "Experiments in Wording Questions: II" (1941)

(4) **Child Psychology:** "This dovetails with new research led by the psychologist Christopher J. Bryan, who finds that for moral behaviors, nouns work better than verbs. To get 3 to 6 year-olds to help with a task, rather than inviting them 'to help,' it was 22 to 29 percent more effective to encourage them to 'be a helper.' Cheating was cut in half when instead of, 'Please don't cheat,' participants were told, 'Please don't be a cheater.' When our actions become a reflection of our character, we lean more heavily toward the moral and generous choices."

—Adam Grant, "Raising a Moral Child" (2014)

(5) **Sex → Gender:** "Everyone laughed when [Justice Ruth Bader Ginsburg] told the story of when she was at Columbia [Law School] in the 1970s and her bright secretary Millicent—who typed her briefs, articles, and speeches about sex discrimination—remarked: 'I have been typing this word, *sex, sex, sex* over and over. Let me tell you, the audience you are addressing, the men you are addressing . . . the first association of that word is not what you are talking about. So I suggest that you use a grammar-book term. Use the term *gender*. It will ward off distracting associations.'"

—Mary Hartnett and Wendy W. Williams writing about Justice Ruth Bader Ginsburg in *My Own Words* (2016) [Note: Justice Ginsburg followed Millicent's advice and used the term "gender discrimination" from then on.]

(6) **Wall Street Game vs. Community Game:** "[Stanford psychologist Lee Ross and his colleagues] conducted a classic 'prisoner's dilemma' scenario with a group of participants. This scenario is one in which two prisoners each are given, separately, the options of cooperating with one another by staying silent, or betraying the other prisoner for a chance at freedom. The catch is that the benefit (or cost) of betrayal versus cooperation is determined by the choice

of the other prisoner—that is, whether one's prisoner's choice is better or worse for his situation depends entirely on what action his counterpart takes.

"The twist to this scenario was that the researchers told participants in one group that they were playing 'the Wall Street Game' and in the other group [they] were told that they were playing 'the Community Game.'

"The results were striking. When participants were told that they were playing the Wall Street Game, 70% of participants acted according to rational self-interest and chose to betray the other prisoner. When participants were told that they were playing the Community Game, however, 70% of the participants chose to cooperate. The key takeaway is that a substantial portion of people decide whether or not to cooperate based on environmental conditions."

—Gerald Kane, "Which Game Are You Playing?" (2014)

(7) **Medicine:** "In recent years, expressions such as 'cancer survivor' have replaced more traditional labels—namely, '[cancer] victim' and '[cancer] patient'—for those diagnosed with cancer. Both the National Coalition for Cancer Survivorship and the Office of Cancer Survivorship at the National Cancer Institute have adopted the more active term 'cancer survivor' as a way to recognize this shift in the cancer culture and in recognition of the unique needs of this growing population. . . . Moreover, research suggests that [an] individual's adoption of a more active cancer-related identity, such as 'cancer survivor,' may have positive consequences for their health and well-being."

—Keith M. Bellizzi and Thomas O. Blank, "Cancer-Related Identity and Positive Affect in Survivors of Prostate Cancer" (2007)

(8) **Gilead:** "I believe he was a saint of some kind. When someone remarked in his hearing that he had lost an eye in the Civil War, he said, 'I prefer to remember that I have kept one.'"

—Marilynne Robinson, *Gilead* (2006)

PRACTICE SECTION

I like the term "decedent." It's as though the man weren't dead, but merely involved in some sort of protracted legal dispute.
　　　　　—Mary Roach, *Stiff: The Curious Lives of Human Cadavers* (2003)

Practice Section #1: Résumé Review

You can define a net two ways, depending on your point of view. Normally, you would say it is a meshed instrument designed to catch fish. But you could, with no great injury to logic, reverse the image and define a net as a jocular lexicographer once did: he called it a collection of holes tied together with string.
　　　　　—Julian Barnes, *Flaubert's Parrot* (1984)

Background

Résumés are a great place to practice the idea of "the words under the words." They give you a chance to frame the same person—yourself—in different ways, to different audiences, for different purposes. As a result, they are a helpful reminder of the two most important questions to ask when sitting down to compose anything from a memo to a contract to a tweet:

- Who is the audience?
- What is the function?

By "function," I mean: What do you want this piece of writing to do? What's the goal? How do you want the people reading it to feel and react? Why are you even writing it in the first place?

Assignment

Find three organizations you would like to work for, whether now or sometime later in your career. Check out each organization's website and other promotional materials. See what kind of language it uses. See what kind of values it communicates. Study the ethos and culture it projects.

Then review your current résumé and ask yourself these questions:

(1) How can I make the words under the words of my résumé match the words under the words of the organization I hope to work for?
(2) How can I describe my education, skills, and experience in a way that will make it easy for the organization to recognize that I would be a great addition to its team?

While creating your three new résumés, spend some time thinking about your rich, varied background. Mine it for possible connections with your target audiences and then make an intentionally long list of your many characteristics and competencies. Deciding which ones should be highlighted to which people is an important part of advocacy. And it will be great training for when you might be asked to do this kind of highlighting on behalf of someone else as well as for when you eventually discover important policies and projects you feel passionate about championing.

* * *

To make this exercise more interesting and helpful, try to pick three organizations that are highly dissimilar. If one organization has an international focus, also pick an organization with a more local focus. If one organization has offices in big cities, also pick an organization that only operates in a single small town. Consider how these differences might affect everything from the projects you decide to describe in your résumé to the items you list in your "Interests" section. The point is to experiment with different versions of yourself and with new ways of saying the same thing.

One more note: don't feel limited to picking only organizations. If there is someone in particular you want to work for one day, create a résumé specifically designed for that person. You'll learn a lot about what it means to tailor information in a purposeful, laser-like way.

* * *

Below are some examples of combinations you might choose based on people and offices graduates of Michigan Law have worked for in the past. Although I want you to be pragmatic when picking your own list, I also want you to stretch yourself a bit. Be creative. Be ambitious. Expand your menu of professional options.

Not every public interest lawyer, for example, stays a public interest lawyer. Nor does every corporate attorney remain at a big firm. Law school is a good time to start imagining alternative futures. But so are other points in your life: when you are visiting a new place, when you are reading a new book, when you are surrounded by people who could give you some helpful advice.

Playing around with your résumé is a pretty low-stakes way to experiment with possible career paths. It can also be quite practical—especially if you end up sending one of your revised résumés out.

Combination #1
Sidley Austin's Chicago office
The US Attorney's Office in Las Vegas
The International Court of Criminal Justice

Combination #2
Montana Legal Services
Ford Motor Company
Chief Justice John Roberts

Combination #3

Davis Polk's Hong Kong office

The Boston Consulting Group

Kobe Bryant (as his agent)

Combination #4

Office of the Public Defender in Columbia, South Carolina

The Minnesota Supreme Court

Google

Practice Section #2: The Name Game

Background

Judge Richard Posner, one of the most influential legal minds to don judicial robes, told his law clerks to call him by his first name. The idea behind this practice, according to Posner's biographer William Domnarski, was to create a work environment that encouraged free thought and open debate.

Assignment

Think about the words under the word "Judge," especially when said by a subordinate. What is it about the term that might make "free thought and open debate" more difficult? Now think of some other contexts:

(1) If you ran a hospital, would you want nurses to call doctors by their first names? Would you want patients to?

(2) How about if you ran a school—would you want third graders to call their teachers by their first names? Would you want high schoolers, undergraduates, or law students to?

(3) Along these same lines, what are the words under the word "Professor"? How can that term be helpful? How can it not?

Think of professors you call by their first names. Now think of the professors you don't.

a. Is there any difference in respect level? Is there any difference in fondness or trust?

b. How about in your willingness to disagree with them?

c. And how do race, age, and gender play into all of this?

To make the assignment more concrete, create a list of five to seven of your past teachers. Include at least one from elementary school, one from middle school, and one from high school. Write out the names completely. Then look it over.

Are there any teachers on it who you would have a hard time calling by their first names? What would be lost if you did? What might be gained?

Practice Section #3: Headlining

Background

At halftime of the 2017 Super Bowl between the New England Patriots and the Atlanta Falcons, the score was pretty lopsided:

Falcons	21
Patriots	3

Midway through the third quarter, the gap was even wider:

Falcons	28
Patriots	3

Yet by the time the final whistle blew, there had been a major reversal. The Patriots ended up with 34 points, the Falcons 28. Two different headlines on ESPN.com that night tried to capture this remarkable turnaround:

- "Historic Comeback Carries Patriots to Super Bowl Victory"
- "Falcons Build Championship Case but Can't Close with Historic Collapse"

Think about the words under the words of the first headline. Which team seems more responsible for the outcome of the game? How about with the second heading? Is that more about divvying out credit or assigning blame?

Assignment

Find a headline in your local paper that describes a game one of the hometown teams just played. It can be a professional game, a college game, or even a high school game.

Once you've found your headline, write it out word for word. Then try to guess how that same game might be framed in the opposing team's local paper. If the Red Sox beat the Yankees, for example, how do you think the headline in the *Boston Globe* would compare with the headline in the *New York Post*? If Michigan beat Ohio State, what do you think each college's campus paper will print?

You can do a version of this exercise with a wide range of other topics. Here are a few:

- political elections
- Supreme Court cases
- invasions, wars, and other military actions

A quick internet search should give you a chance to test the accuracy of your guess.

TWO

The Infinite Power of Grammar

Think of a grammar as an app for converting a cluster of ideas into a string of words. English relies mainly on word order to do this: Dog bites man *is different from* Man bites dog.

—Steven Pinker, "Passive Resistance" (2014)

The Infinite Power of Grammar: Concept

Grammar, which knows how to control even kings.

—Molière, *Les Femmes savantes* (1672)

The order in which our sentences unfold or hit the reader is entirely within our control. Even better, syntactical choices can help us increase the precision of our writing, bringing what we say into sharper focus, even if we don't have a mental thesaurus.

—Brooks Landon, *Building Great Sentences* (2013)

At Cornell University, my professor of European literature, Vladimir Nabokov, changed the way I read and the way I write. Words could paint pictures, I learned from him. Choosing the right word, and the right word order, he illustrated, could make an enormous difference in conveying an image or an idea.

—Justice Ruth Bader Ginsburg,
"Ruth Bader Ginsburg's Advice for Living" (2016)

Being good with words means more than choosing the right words; it also means choosing the right word order. The formal term for this choice is "syntax." But perhaps a better description comes from a 1976 essay by Joan Didion called "Why I Write."

In it, Didion draws a helpful parallel between the arrangement of a photograph and the arrangement of a sentence. "To shift the structure of a sentence," she explains, "alters the meaning of that sentence, as definitely and inflexibly as the position of the camera alters the meaning of the object photographed." Didion refers to this phenomenon as grammar's "infinite power." The phrase captures just how transformative word order can be.

Imagine, for example, you are preparing to move. Your boxes are packed. Your rugs are rolled. Your U-Haul is all gassed up and ready to go. Now you just need somebody to help you lug the heavy stuff. So you text a friend and receive one of two responses:

"I would love to help, but my parents are in town."

or,

"My parents are in town, but I would love to help."

In many ways, both responses are the same. Both contain the same marks of punctuation: a comma and a period. Both contain the same number of words: 11. Both even contain the same exact words. The only difference is the order of those words. The only difference is syntax.

Yet that difference, in this case and many others, can be substantial. It's the difference between your request being met with what seems like a no ("I would love to help, but my parents are in town.") or it being met with what seems like a yes ("My parents are in town, but I would love to help."). It's the difference between a job offer ("More than 500 people applied for this job, but we would really like to hire you.") and a job snub ("We would really like to hire you, but more than 500 applied for this job."). It's even the difference between the end to a good first date ("I am leaving the country next week, but I would love to do this again.") and the end to a dud ("I would love to do this again, but I am leaving the country next week.").

Learn this difference. Learn the infinite power of grammar. Remember that the order of words can be flipped and shifted, that new insights are often triggered by new configurations. Yes, you should edit by deleting words. Yes, you should edit by adding words. But you should also edit by rearranging them. Said differently: Keep the content—just change the location.

Doing this will help you create clearer, more effective sequences and combinations. It will also teach you not to treat as fixed and immovable any structure you write or inherit.

Confrontation Clause

Take this sentence from a case involving the Confrontation Clause, which is the part of the Sixth Amendment that gives criminal defendants the right to cross-examine—or "confront"—the witnesses who testify against them:

> The district court erred when it admitted out-of-court statements from an unidentified declarant implicating Mr. Richard in the crime in violation of Mr. Richard's Sixth Amendment rights.

A lot of things can be done to improve that sentence, which comes from a brief written by two law students in the University of Michigan's Federal Appellate Clinic. We might begin, however, by simply reordering the words. The important thing to stress in this case is that Mr. Richard's Sixth Amendment rights were violated. So why not start with that directly?

> In violation of Mr. Richard's Sixth Amendment rights, the district court erred when it admitted out-of-court statements from an unidentified declarant implicating Mr. Richard in the crime.

No word was added to the sentence the students originally wrote. No word was removed. But it is already much more readable and compelling.

A similar transformation can be performed on this hilariously misguided sentence collected as an example of bad writing in *Plain English for Lawyers* by Richard Wydick.

> The defendant was arrested for fornicating under a little-used state statute.

To avoid the impression that the defendant used the statute as a blanket and was caught actually having sex *beneath* it, we might invert the sentence.

> Under a little-used state statute, the defendant was arrested for fornicating.

The word "under" may continue to create problems for some readers. But the contrast between the original version and the edited version nevertheless shows how word order, just like word choice, really can transform the clarity and meaning of a sentence.

The magazine *The Economist* has figured this out. Playing with the common phrase "Great minds think alike," it created a clever ad campaign out of the following inversion: "Great minds like a think."

This slogan perfectly targets *The Economist*'s audience while at the same time communicating a lot about the magazine's ethos: witty, worldly, intellectual, and also a bit irreverent. It's an excellent piece of advocacy. And all the magazine did was rearrange some words.

James Joyce

Of course, rearranging words isn't always an easy task. An anecdote about the literary giant James Joyce demonstrates this point. The anecdote has been told in many places, including the memoir of another literary giant, Stephen King. It's a good reminder of how much care and energy the best writers put into finding the right syntax and taking full advantage of the infinite power of grammar.

The anecdote begins with a visit from one of Joyce's friends. Joyce doesn't get up to greet the friend. Instead, he stays slumped over his writing desk, pouty and dejected after an apparently frustrating day of writing. The friend asks Joyce what's wrong. Joyce doesn't respond. The friend then guesses it might have something to do with Joyce's literary output that day. So he asks Joyce how many words Joyce wrote since starting in the morning.

"Seven," Joyce says.

Aware that Joyce is the kind of wordsmith who labors over every word he writes, the friend tries to be encouraging. "Seven is pretty good," he says, "at least for you."

"Yes, I suppose it is," Joyce says, not entirely consoled. "But I still don't know what order they go in!"

* * *

You'll probably want to avoid Joyce's level of obsessiveness. You have deadlines to meet, assignments to start, sanity to preserve. That said, build in some time, whenever you write, to play around with the infinite power of grammar. Given the importance of syntax—in contracts; in advertisements; in emails, articles, and all other forms of writing—you can't afford not to. As Didion says elsewhere in "Why I Write," with characteristic brevity and force, "The arrangement of the words matters."

QUESTIONS SECTION

Ask not what your country can do for you; ask what you can do for your country.
—John F. Kennedy, Inaugural Address (1961)

The Infinite Power of Grammar: Questions*

(1) **The Syntax of Sentencing:** Suppose you are representing a woman convicted of a crime. We'll call her Ms. Hester. When it comes time to sentence Ms. Hester, the judge could say one of either two things:

a. "Look, Ms. Hester, I think you are genuinely sorry for the harm you have caused, and I think you are also really committed to being a productive member of society—but the crime you committed warrants a significant punishment."

b. "Look, Ms. Hester, the crime you committed warrants a significant punishment—but I think you are genuinely sorry for the harm you have caused, and I think you are also really committed to being a productive member of society."

Which statement do you think your client is hoping to hear?

---

* For answers, see page 220 of Appendix C.

(2) **The Syntax of Sports:** Buddy Ryan is famous among football fans for creating the "46 defense," a positioning scheme so dominant that many consider the 1985 Chicago Bears team that used it to be the best ever assembled. Yet there is a way to think of Ryan's innovation as a simple move of syntax. He didn't add any players to the 11 each team is allowed on the field at a time. Nor did he remove any players. All he did was rearrange how they lined up.

Can you think of other examples of how syntax might be applied to nonwriting tasks?

- What about interior decorating?
- What about food presentation?
- What about the way a courtroom or chemistry lab is set up?
- Is there a syntax of science? A syntax of engineering? A syntax of management, medicine, or math?

(3) **The Syntax of Retail:** Gordon Segal and his wife Carole opened their first "Crate & Barrel" store in 1962 in Chicago. Fifty-five years later, with annual sales at the company exceeding one billion dollars, Gordon told NPR's Guy Raz the story of how the store got its name. Because Gordon and Carole didn't have any money to decorate their first shop, they simply stacked the merchandise on the big barrels and crates that suppliers had used to ship them their products.

Then one day, two weeks before the official opening of the store, a friend came by. He saw the barrels. He saw the crates. And so he suggested to Carole that the still-unnamed store be called "Barrel & Crate."

Carole liked the idea but told Gordon that they should make one slight syntactic switch. The name shouldn't be "Barrel & Crate"; it should be "Crate & Barrel."

It's been called that ever since.

- Below is a list of companies whose correct names I have syntactically switched. Fill in the blank with the missing part of the name and then write the whole thing the correct way.

Example: Jerry & _____

Answer: Jerry & Ben's → Ben & Jerry's

Fitch & _____

Gamble & _____

Deluca & _____

Decker & _____

Poor's & _____

Gabana & _____

Wesson & _____

- Do any of these names sound better to you in reverse order than they do in their normal order?
- There are at least two major brands whose names are immune to syntactic switching. One makes products such as Listerine, Band-Aids, and Tylenol. Another is a kind of candy. Can you identify them? (Or any other business with the same immunity.)

(4) **Child Custody:** A student attorney at the University of Michigan Law School was representing a Colombian mother in a custody dispute. The student originally wrote this sentence to help persuade the judge that the mother was not a flight risk, despite the (groundless) protestations of her husband:

> Other than Mr. Macondo's unsubstantiated claims, there is no evidence that Ms. Macondo will flee to Colombia, a country she was desperate to leave, with José.

Suppose you think it is a little confusing and awkward to put "with José" at the end of the sentence. Without adding or deleting words, how could you rearrange the sentence so that it ends with "desperate to leave"?

(5) **The Syntax of Style:** A civil war general named Ambrose Burnside has become famous for the way he styled his facial hair: long strips of hair joined as a mustache but with his chin clean-shaven. The modern name for the long strips of hair is an inversion of the syllables in Burnside's name akin to an inversion in syntax. What is it?

EXAMPLES SECTION

All syntax can do, and it is a very great deal, is to make the right word shine to its best advantage, as brightly as possible and in just the right place, set off from others or clustered with them.

—Virginia Tufte, Grammar as Style (1971)

The Infinite Power of Grammar: Examples

(1) **Point of View:** "[H]er breast grazed my elbow, or my elbow grazed her breast, depending on your perspective."

—Colson Whitehead, Sag Harbor (2010)

(2) **Poet Laureate:** "[Billy] Collins' revisions suggest an orderly process of refinement and improvement. They continued, as you can see if you consult the final version of the poem as published under the title 'In the Evening,' in *The New Delta Review*. Almost every line has been changed from this manuscript, usually in subtle ways. For example, 'I pick up a knife and an onion' has become, 'I pick up an onion and a knife.' Better, no?"

—Ben Yagoda, The Sound on the Page: Great
Writers Talk About Style (2005)

(3) **Google:** "When the company was smaller, we drew a public distinction between two levels of director, where the more junior role would be titled as 'Director, Engineering,' and the more senior role would be 'Engineering Director.' We found that even such a subtle distinction in the word order of the title caused our people to fixate on the difference between the two levels. So we eliminated the difference."

—Laszlo Bock, Work Rules! Insights From Inside Google
That Will Transform How You Live and Lead (2015)

(4) **Photographer Ansel Adams:** "The reason [Ansel Adams] is important to us, as I think he is, is because he was a good artist. On his best days, he was a terrific artist. And he found some way to put together the fragments of the world in a way that transformed them into a picture. In the same way that a poet uses the same dictionaries that the rest of us do—all the words are in there, all the words in the poem are [in the dictionary]. It is just a matter of taking a few of them and putting them in the right order. That's all there is to it. . . . A good picture does something like that."

—John Szarkowski, in *American Experience: Ansel Adams* (2002)

(5) **Legal Scholar Geoffrey Hazard:** "The word processor now provides wonderful flexibility in repositioning sentence elements. I often put the key words and phrases on the screen without knowing their proper sequence and move them around to find what seems the best fit."

—Geoffrey Hazard, "How I Write" (1993)

(6) **Ruining a Cake:** "Cooking recipes are also 'syntactic descriptions': American cookbooks even follow the two-part format by first listing the ingredients selected and then giving the order in which they need to be mixed. Just as sentences can be selectionally grammatical but ungrammatical in order or ungrammatical even by selection, a cake can also be ruined because the right ingredients have been mixed in the wrong order."

—Edith Moravcsik, *An Introduction to Syntax: Fundamentals of Syntactic Analysis* (2006)

(7) **Choreography:** "At times I've envisioned language as a body with its own surge and rhythms and whims, other times as a diaphanous garment that both hides and reveals. But always I see grammar as the choreographer of our language, coordinating the movements

of our baffling, fumbling urge to express, to give voice to the ineffable."

—Constance Hale, *Sin and Syntax: How to Craft Wickedly Effective Prose* (2001)

(8) **Stephen Colbert:** "And to combat these Grade 'A' bad eggs, we've created The Greatest Criminal Justice System on Earth as seen eight times a day on TNT in the various *Laws & Orderses*. Mind you, the police—'Order'—technic-ally do their job before the prosecutors apply the 'Law.' So it should really be called 'Order & Law.' Show creator Dick Wolf really shanked that one."

—Stephen Colbert, *America Again: Re-becoming the Greatness We Never Weren't* (2012)

PRACTICE SECTION

I like the idea that every page in every book can have a gem on it. It's probably what I love most about writing—that words can be used in a way that's like a child playing in a sandpit, rearranging things, swapping them around.

—Markus Zusak, author interview in the
anniversary edition of *The Book Thief* (2007)

Practice Section #1: Interrupting Elements

Background

The University of Virginia used to have a website to help writers and writing teachers. On it, several principles for clear and direct communication were listed. One aligned particularly well with the idea of the infinite power of grammar and the helpful edits that can be made through subtle shifts in syntax. Advising writers to avoid interrupting their subjects and verbs with long phrases and clauses, the site explained that "when readers do not see a verb right after a subject, the sentence is probably more difficult than it has to be."

It then recommended shifting an interrupting element to either the end or the beginning of the sentence, depending on where the element fits better. Here's the example the site offered:

> **Original Version:** Some scientists, because they write in a style that is so impersonal and objective, do not communicate with laypeople easily.
>
> **Clearer and More Direct Version:** Some scientists do not communicate with laypeople easily, because they write in a style that is so impersonal and objective.

The advice reinforces a broader principle on the site: "Get to verbs quickly." Readers typically don't like to have to wait to figure out the main action of the sentence. They get confused. They get distracted. Their brains hurt.

I say that to my law students all the time. "Don't make my brain hurt. It's not going to make me like you or be persuaded by your points. And I am pretty sure the judge (or client) is going to feel the same way."

Assignment

Take at least three pages of something you have written recently. Read it carefully. Using a blue pen, circle the subject in each sentence. Using the same blue pen, circle the verb that goes with that subject. Then with a red pen, underline any interrupting element; in other words, underline any segment of the sentence in which the verb does not come directly after the subject but is instead separated—you might even think of it as being delayed—by an intervening phrase or clause.*

To give you a sense of what you'll be looking for, here is a different view of the original sentence from the Virginia website:

(subject)	(main verb)
Some scientists	do not communicate with laypeople easily.

(interrupting element)
because they write in a style that is so impersonal and objective

It is possible that you will have multiple subjects and multiple verbs in your sentences. The example from Virginia does:

- First subject: "Some scientists" → First verb: "do not communicate"
- Second subject: "they" → Second verb: "write"

---

* Many of my students forgo pens and instead use the various highlighting devices included in Microsoft Word and similar programs. That works too. Just be sure to keep using one color for the subject and verb and a different color for the interrupting element, if there is one.

In that case, use one color pen for the first subject-verb pair and a different color pen for any additional subject-verb pairs. But always mark interrupting elements in red. After you're done, these elements should stand out unmistakably.

You don't have to move or delete every interrupting element you find. Some can be quite useful—for emphasis, for rhythm, for a break from the monotony created when all you do is use the same straightforward syntax. Toward the end of each semester, I encourage my students to experiment with interrupting elements. I tell them that interrupting elements can add variety and sophistication to their writing, that interrupting elements are used all the time by master stylists like James Baldwin, Virginia Woolf, Edith Wharton, Edward Gibbon, Marcel Proust, and Gabriel García Márquez.

But the point of the current assignment is to focus on simply becoming aware of interrupting elements. Then you can decide which are worth keeping.

Practice Section #2: Short to Long

Background

The Virginia site had another helpful way to think about syntax and how it can be used to avoid making your reader's brain hurt. They called it "Short to Long."

A sentence consists of more than its subjects and verbs, the site explained. "At a 'higher' level of analysis, a sentence also consists of bundles of information. Some bundles are [short] and easily unpacked for their information; others are long and complex, and readers have to work harder to unpack them." The suggestion is that it's more reader friendly to start with shorter bundles of information. Longer, complex bundles should be saved for the end. The site offered the following succinct summation: "Put short bundles of information before long bundles of information."

Here is one of the examples:

Original (Long to Short): At Hunter LAN Technologies, provision to our customers in a timely fashion of technically accurate, readable information about products <u>is our goal</u>.

Rewrite (Short to Long): At Hunter LAN Technologies, <u>our goal is to provide</u> technically accurate, readable information about our products to our customers in a timely fashion.

I have underlined the verb phrase in each sentence to highlight how the key edit when transforming a "Long to Short" structure into a "Short to Long" structure is to shift the main verb to the beginning of the sentence. You want the reader to be able to get to that verb as quickly as possible. Dillydallying will impede comprehension.

Another way to put this point is to echo advice F. Scott Fitzgerald once offered in a letter to his daughter Frances, an aspiring writer who would later become a journalist for the *Washington Post* and the *New Yorker*: All good writing depends on "verbs carrying a sentence," Fitzgerald told her. "They make sentences move."

What the folks at Virginia seem to be saying is that the longer you delay that movement—the longer you make readers wait to figure out what a sentence is trying to communicate—the more likely they are to get bored, confused, distracted, even annoyed. Attention spans are short. Patience withers. Your main idea shouldn't be a mystery.

There are exceptions, of course. Sometimes you'll want to build suspense into your sentences. You'll want them to unfold and develop with every new clause and thought, like a book that gets better with each successive chapter. But we're not ready for exceptions yet. We're still building our base of default settings—which is exactly what principles like "Short to Long" and "interrupting elements" are. They're defaults. They're not immutable laws of the writing universe. They're not prescriptions you absolutely must follow, regardless of the audience or medium. In many situations, you can—and should—opt out of them.

But first, you need to understand what you are opting out of. You need to be able to recognize the short and long elements in sentences and then evaluate when it is good to start short and go long, and when you want to instead start long and go short.

Assignment

Take out the colored pens you used to complete the interrupting elements exercise. Then select three pages of writing. The writing can be something you have composed, or it can be something another person has composed. Academic papers are good sources of "Long to Short" sentences, as are all manner of legal writing: briefs, contracts, judicial opinions—pretty much anything written by someone with a JD. You can also find them in business plans, office memos, and application essays.

Once you settle on your sample, go through every sentence carefully. Underline in red any sentences that strike you as "Long to Short." Underline in blue any that strike you as "Short to Long."

Remember that the placement of the main verb—by which I mean the verb that communicates the principal action of the sentence—will be your best guide to noticing the difference. If the main verb comes more than halfway through the sentence, count it as "Long to Short" and underline it in red. If the main verb comes less than halfway through the sentence, count it as "Short to Long" and underline it in blue.

There may be some close calls. That's okay. The goal is not taxonomical precision. You are simply trying to train yourself to spot a type of sentence that may cause readers more trouble than it's worth.

* * *

Here are some additional examples to help calibrate your "Long to Short" radar and show you how to produce something closer to "Short to Long." The first comes from a research memo written by a law student. Notice what happens to the phrase "a two-part test":

Original (Long to Short): The issue of whether the city has potential contractual liability to third-party beneficiaries injured by a dangerous condition in the parking lot is subject to <u>a two-part test</u>.

Rewrite (Short to Long): <u>A two-part test</u> determines whether the city has potential contractual liability to third-party beneficiaries injured by a dangerous condition in the parking lot.

Once you complete that initial step of switching from "Long to Short" to "Short to Long," it becomes easier to edit the sentence even more:

Further Rewrite (Short to Long): <u>A two-part test</u> determines whether the city is liable to third-party beneficiaries injured by a dangerous condition in the parking lot.

Here is a second example from the same memo:

Original (Long to Short): In *Koenig v. City of South Haven*, parents of a teenager who suffered injuries that ultimately proved fatal after a wave swept her off a pier and into the lake <u>sued</u> the city.

Rewrite (Short to Long): In *Koenig v. City of South Haven*, parents of a teenager <u>sued</u> the city after a wave swept the teenager off a pier and caused injuries that ultimately proved fatal.

A final example comes from a judicial opinion:

Original (Long to Short): Decker's successful argument that his claim is not barred by res judicata because its state-court version was dismissed on failure-to-administratively-exhaust grounds <u>raises</u> an unresolved question for the court: should this case also be dismissed?

Rewrite (Short to Long): An unresolved question <u>is raised</u> by Decker's successful argument that his claim is not barred by res judicata because its state-court version was dismissed on failure-to-administratively-exhaust grounds: should this case also be dismissed?

A Note About Passive Constructions

Some of you may have read the rewrite of the judicial opinion and shuddered at its use of a passive construction, the way it puts the focus on the thing being raised ("An unresolved question is raised . . .") instead of on the thing doing the raising. Perhaps you even heard, ringing in your ears, the voice of one of your former teachers telling you that passive constructions should be avoided at all costs.

I recommend you quiet that voice.

You don't have to quiet it entirely. You don't have to silence it. More than likely, your teacher's admonition came from a good place, a place that recognizes that active constructions are often preferable to passive constructions, that they can give your sentences a directness and vigor that passive constructions frequently don't.

Passive constructions can be droopy. They can be sluggish. Worse, they can allow people to duck responsibility. "I'm sorry that your nose was broken" is a pretty lame apology from someone who just punched you in the face. "I'm sorry I broke your nose" is both more active and more admirable.

At the same time, however, a categorical ban against passive constructions is like a categorical ban against using your left hand. You may be able to get by without your left hand in many situations. You don't normally need it, for example, to shake someone else's hand, or to salute, or to perform the Pledge of Allegiance. But eventually, if you decide you can never use it, you'll unnecessarily limit yourself and forgo a lot of creative versatility.

The psychologist Steven Pinker describes this versatility in "Passive Resistance," an essay that argues that active constructions aren't always the best choice. The author of several books on language and the chair of the Usage Panel of the *American Heritage Dictionary*, Pinker suggests that passive constructions are supremely useful when you want to put the spotlight not on the doers of a particular action but on the recipients. Think of the phrase "all men are created equal" from the Declaration of Independence. The spotlight is on "all men" and the equality each shares. It is not on the being who did the creating. The same is true of the document's very next clause, which begins "that they are endowed by."

Pinker doesn't use the Declaration of Independence to support his point—but he could. He could also use skillful bits of legal writing. Below are two passages from briefs written by Jeff Fisher, one of the country's top appellate advocates and the codirector of Stanford's Supreme Court Litigation Clinic. The first passage comes from *Crawford v. Washington*, a case in which Fisher, using arguments developed by the University of Michigan's Richard Friedman, persuaded the Supreme Court to radically transform the way hearsay evidence is treated in criminal trials. I have underlined the passive part:

> Applying this traditional, testimonial understanding of the Confrontation Clause, the proper result here is clear: [Crawford's] confrontation rights were violated because the State introduced a nontestifying accomplice's custodial examination implicating him in the charged offense.

You could make that passive part active. You could write "The State violated Crawford's confrontation rights." But then the spotlight would be on the State. Fisher, with good reason, kept it on his client (Crawford). The passive part gave Fisher the flexibility to do that. The passive part was purposeful.

Fisher did something similar in *United States v. O'Brien*, another case he won in the Supreme Court. This time, however, he used a passive construction to put the spotlight not on a person but on the absence of an action. In fact, he used three of them right in a row:

> When one of the guards fled, the men promptly abandoned the attempted robbery. O'Brien drove Burgess and Quirk away in the minivan. <u>No shots were fired, no money was taken, and no one was injured.</u>

A version of this passive trifecta was picked up and used in the Court's majority opinion, which eight of the nine justices signed and Justice Anthony Kennedy penned. "[O'Brien, Burgess, and Quirk] abandoned the robbery and fled without taking any money," Kennedy wrote in his description of the facts of the case. "<u>No shots were fired, and no one was injured.</u>"

* * *

Does this mean that if you use passive constructions, the Supreme Court and other key decision-makers will be persuaded by your arguments?

No. It doesn't mean that at all. In the Supreme Court and most every place else, sound strategy still favors active constructions. No style guide I know comes out against them. And particularly if you are just starting out at a new job, in a new class, or with a new boss, you should keep in mind that frolics into the passive may be judged harshly. So here's some advice I give my students. It has three parts:

- **Part 1:** Know the difference between passive constructions and active constructions. Writing in the *Los Angeles Times*, grammar columnist June Casagrande explains it the following way:

> The passive voice, sometimes called simply "the passive," describes a very specific relationship between a transitive verb and its object. For example, "coffee" is the object of the verb "made"

in "Joe made coffee." This is active voice because the doer of the action is also the subject of the sentence.

But what if we said instead, "Coffee was made by Joe"? Now the coffee, the thing receiving the action of the verb, is the grammatical subject of the sentence, upstaging the person who's actually performing that action.

That's passive voice. It takes the object of a verb and makes it the grammatical subject of the sentence by using a form of the verb "be" paired with what's called the passive participle, which is identical to the past participle.

The result often takes the form "Blank was blanked by blank."

- **Part 2:** Don't slip into passive constructions accidentally. They are likely to bring with them a bunch of extra words, each of which may weigh down and de-energize your sentences. They also sometimes make it harder for readers to figure out what you are trying to say. Which is why articles in various science journals—including two of the most prestigious ones—have at different points encouraged writers to use active constructions instead:

> Nature journals prefer authors to write in the active voice ("we performed the experiment . . .") as experience has shown that readers find concepts and results to be conveyed more clearly if written directly.
>
> —"How to Write a Paper:
> Writing for a *Nature* Journal" (*Nature*)

> Use active voice when suitable, particularly when necessary for correct syntax (e.g., "To address this possibility, we constructed a λZap library . . ." not "To address this possibility, a λZap library was constructed . . .").
>
> —"Some Notes on *Science* Style" (*Science*)

- **Part 3:** Do use passive constructions purposefully, particularly when trying to keep a certain person, idea, object, or nonaction in the spotlight, as Jeff Fisher did in those two Supreme Court briefs and as skilled writers do *all* the time.

If you are worried that your purposeful use of a passive construction will be interpreted as an accidental use of passive construction, a further step would be to use a comment bubble, Post-it Note, or some other annotation to tell your teacher or supervisor that your choice was deliberate. Even if she ultimately changes the construction back to active, at least she'll know you are someone who thinks carefully, even strategically, about the words you choose. That's unlikely to hurt your career prospects.

THREE

The Rule of Three

The Good, the Bad, and the Ugly

—Clint Eastwood movie

The Rule of Three: Concept

"All right," he said at last. "Things always come in three."
—Jeanne Desy, "The Princess Who Stood on Her Own Two Feet"(2015)

I was simmering, simmering, simmering; Emerson brought me to a boil.
—Walt Whitman

Stop, drop, and roll.

—fire safety instruction

There is an attractive rhythm that comes from ordering information in threes. The Supreme Court uses this rhythm. At the start of each session, the marshal of the Court announces "the Honorable, the Chief Justice, and the Associate Justices of the Supreme Court of the United States. Oyez! Oyez! Oyez!" The marshal doesn't say "Oyez!" The marshal doesn't say "Oyez! Oyez!" The marshal says "Oyez! Oyez! Oyez!" That third "Oyez" completes the sound of a comforting syntactic set.

This sound structure rules the world of real estate as well. The mantra of the market is not "Location." Nor is it "Location. Location." It's "Location. Location. Location." Just as the mantra of the football team at the University of Michigan is not "The team" or even "The team. The team." It's "The team. The team. The team." Taken from a speech given in 1983 by Bo Schembechler, one of Michigan's many legendary coaches, the three-part phrase can be seen on posters all over campus, as well as on T-shirts, hats, and other memorabilia worn by fans and alumni across the country. It's one of the university's biggest exports.

Examples from other realms abound, emphasizing a range of ideas, from funny to disconcerting:

> **Food:** "We obsess over every ingredient.
> "We obsess over every ingredient.
> "We obsess over every ingredient."
> —Chipotle billboard campaign in Chicago

Music: Q. "Pardon me, sir, how do I get to Carnegie Hall?"
A. "Practice. Practice. Practice."

—popular joke

The Brady Bunch: "All I hear all day long at school is how great Marcia is at this and how wonderful Marcia is at that. Marcia! Marcia! Marcia!"

—Jan Brady (whining)

Divorce: "I divorce you. I divorce you. I divorce you."
—ancient Islamic custom practiced in India where men could divorce their wives just by saying "I divorce you" three times. (Women were not given the same power.)*

Poets, novelists, and other professional writers are particularly keen followers of this apparent "Rule of Three." In 1835, for example, Lord Alfred Tennyson wrote a poem to try to capture the pain and loneliness he felt after the death of his good friend Arthur Hallam, a fellow poet and university student at Cambridge who died of an unexpected cerebral hemorrhage when only 22 years old. Tennyson called the poem "Break, Break, Break." He also included those words at the start of the first and the last stanza.

Over 150 years later, the Japanese writer Haruki Murakami published the novel *Dansu, Dansu, Dansu*, which has been translated as *Dance, Dance, Dance*. And for younger readers, there is Pat Mora's Spanish version of *The Crow and the Pitcher*, a tale of water and ingenuity

---

* In 2017, the India Supreme Court struck down the provision that permitted this so-called instant divorce. For more on that decision, check out "India's Supreme Court Strikes Down 'Instant Divorce' for Muslims" by *New York Times* reporters Jeffrey Gettleman & Suhasini Raj (Aug. 22, 2017, available at https://www.nytimes.com/2017/08/22/world/asia/india-muslim-divorce-triple-talaq.html).

taken from one of Aesop's fables. Mora calls her version *Agua, Agua, Agua*. The Rule of Three, it seems, is helpfully multilingual.

Or how about this passage from John Cheever's 1954 short story "The Five-Forty-Eight." A master of dialogue, of capturing the meter and mood of ordinary speech, Cheever uses the Rule of Three twice in a very compact space:

> "Oh, no," she said. "<u>No, no, no</u>." She put her white face so close to his ear that he could feel her warm breath on his cheek. "Don't do that," she whispered. "Don't try and escape me. I have a pistol and I'll have to kill you and I don't want to. All I want to do is to talk with you. Don't move or I'll kill you. <u>Don't, don't, don't!</u>"

Emma Cline achieves a similar effect in "Northeast Regional," a short story she published in 2017. This time, however, the Rule of Three is used only once, and the words are imagined to be inside somebody else's head:

> She had tried her best to be a good sport. That was the phrase he was sure was circling down at the bottom of her thought's stern ticker tape: <u>be a good sport</u> <u>be a good sport</u> <u>be a good sport</u>.

Both Cheever's story and Cline's appeared in the *New Yorker*, a magazine whose ad campaign for its digital content shows that the possibilities of the Rule of Three extend beyond just straight repetition: "Every story. Every issue. Every device."

The ad doesn't stop after one item ("Every story.") or after two ("Every story. Every issue."). It also doesn't stretch to include four items ("Every story. Every issue. Every device. Every day."). That might be overkill. Instead, it settles on three items: "Every story. Every issue. Every device." The Rule of Three is the advertising sweet spot.

All of the following organizations agree:

Target (Gift Card): "No fees. No expiration. No kidding."

Stanford Business School: "Change lives. Change organizations. Change the world."

Buffalo Wild Wings: "Wings. Beer. Sports."

Khan Academy: "For free. For everyone. Forever."

Southwest Airlines: "New Year. New Adventure. New Sale."

US Marine Corps: "The Few. The Proud. The Marines."

Short, Short, Kind of Long

Notice the subtle shift in the last example, the one from the US Marine Corps. If you focus on the number of syllables in each item in the list—"The Few" (two syllables), "The Proud" (two syllables), "The Marines" (three syllables)—you'll see the shift follows this structure: "short, short, kind of long." A clearer example comes from the most famous line in the Declaration of Independence.

life,   liberty,   and the pursuit of happiness

(short)   **(short)**   *(kind of long)*

The words "life" and "liberty" are both under three syllables in length. They're short. By comparison, the phrase "the pursuit of happiness" is kind of long. So it goes at the end of the list. As creators of everything from movie taglines to children's stories to world-changing political documents understand, the last slot in the Rule of Three is often reserved for lengthier, more complex material.

The first draft of the Declaration, for example, received a lot of edits from other founding fathers. Some of these edits Jefferson disagreed with so strongly that he called them "mutilations" and "depredations." But none of the edits ever suggested he change "life, liberty, and the pursuit of happiness" to "life, the pursuit of happiness, and liberty" or to "the pursuit of happiness, liberty, and life." None tinkered with the structure of the Rule of Three.

Same, Same, Kind of Different

A more general way to think about this three-part structure is "same, same, kind of different." The first two items in the list share something in common. Maybe they start with the same letter. Maybe they contain the same word. Maybe they each have a common rhythm, syntax, or shape. But then you get to the third item, and the pattern breaks.

A good example is "life, liberty, and estate." The phrase—which some have linked to Jefferson's own "life, liberty, and the pursuit of happiness"—comes from John Locke's *Second Treatise of Government* published in 1689. Notice that Locke's phrase doesn't fit the structure of "short, short, kind of long." The word "life" is one syllable; the word "liberty" is three syllables; the word "estate" is two. Which means one of the slots reserved for a "short" item is actually longer than the slot for the "kind of long" item.

But if you focus on the alliteration in the first two items—"life" and "liberty"—you'll see that it does fit the structure of "same, same, kind of different." The first word ("life") starts with the letter "l"; the second word ("liberty") also starts with the letter "l"; but then the pattern breaks when you get to the third item ("estate"). Ward Farnsworth, the dean of the University of Texas Law School, has a nice way of describing how changing up a rhetorical pattern can have a pleasing and persuasive effect, particularly when the change comes after two examples of the same thing. In these circumstances, he writes in *Classical English Rhetoric*, "the ear welcomes the relief."

I am not sure that the marketing team at Costco Wholesale has read Farnsworth's book. But they seem to understand the phenomenon he identifies, at least judging by a promotional poster that appeared in the company's Ann Arbor store in the spring of 2018.

No headaches.   No hassles.   Just savings.
(same)   **(same)**   (*kind of different*)

The same appears to be true of the folks at Sidley Austin LLP, one of the largest law firms in the world. As of the summer of 2018, the firm's website showcased this tagline:

Talent.   Teamwork.   Results.
(same)   **(same)**   (*kind of different*)

Big Law gets the Rule of Three.

Phrasemakers

The focus of this chapter has been on phrases because if you learn how to create effective phrases, you can learn how to create effective sentences; and if you learn how to create effective sentences, you can learn how to create effective paragraphs; and if you learn how to create effective paragraphs, you can produce some really great writing.

Here, for example, is Justice Oliver Wendell Holmes Jr. using the "short, short, kind of long" version of the Rule of Three in his celebrated dissent in *Lochner v. New York*, a piece of writing Judge Richard Posner called, back in 1998, "the greatest judicial opinion of the last hundred years":

> The liberty of the citizen to do as he likes so long as he does not interfere with the liberty of others to do the same, which has been a shibboleth for some well-known writers, is interfered with by school laws, by the Post Office, by every state or municipal institution which takes his money for purposes thought desirable, whether he likes it or not. The Fourteenth Amendment does not enact Mr. Herbert Spencer's *Social Statics*.

And here is William Finnegan using it in *Barbarian Days: A Surfing Life*, which won the 2016 Pulitzer Prize. Finnegan shows that the

Rule of Three can do more than help craft a single sentence; it can also help craft an entire string of sentences.

> Nobody bothered me. Nobody vibed me. It was the opposite of my life at school.

A final example comes from an opening statement in the trial of Timothy McVeigh, who was convicted of blowing up a federal building in downtown Oklahoma City in April of 1995. More than 150 people were killed in the blast. Trying to convey to the jury that none of the victims could have suspected the terrible fate that awaited them when they each got up that morning, the prosecutor in the case, Joe Hartzler, does exactly what Finnegan does in *Barbarian Days*—he uses the Rule of Three to craft a string of sentences:

> The sun was shining. Flowers were blooming. It was springtime in Oklahoma City.

Later, Hartzler returns to the same structure, this time employing a kind of Rule of Three in Reverse: instead of using the order "short, short, kind of long," he uses the order "long, long, kind of short."

> We'll present a lot of evidence against McVeigh. (**long**)
> We'll try to make your decision ultimately easy. (**long**)
> That's our goal. (*kind of short*)

Notice, however, that "long, long, kind of short" is still "same, same, kind of different." Or as Farnsworth might put it: "same, same, relief."

Visible Speech

Hartzler's opening statement is a good place to end the concept part of this chapter. That his statement started out as a something written and ended up as something spoken highlights the connection between writing and speaking. Most people preparing to give a speech understand this connection. They write out what they are going to say beforehand, even if the plan is to eventually deliver their remarks without any notes.

Not enough people, however, realize the connection is also important when the end product will remain on a page. Writing, the linguist John DeFrancis has suggested, is "visible speech." It is a way of communicating sound and meaning through symbols. Neglect that sound, neglect the possibility for rhythm and melody in sentences, the chance to use pace and harmony, tone and expressiveness—neglect all those musical elements and you neglect much of what gives words their value. As the poet Robert Frost remarked in a letter to a friend in 1914, "The ear is the only true writer and the only true reader."

The next chapter explores the idea of visible speech a little further, returning to the writing of Frost to introduce a link both he and many other writers have identified: the link between sound and sense. For now, spend some time with the other sections of this chapter: the questions section, the example section, and the practice section. They offer a chance to practice the neat combination of sound and sense generated by the Rule of Three, as do these lines from a couple of Frost's own poems:

What country'd be the one to dominate
By character, by tongue, by native trait.
   (same)   **(same)**   *(different)*

—"Dedication" (1961)

The faded earth, the heavy sky,
    (same)   **(same)**
The beauties she so truly sees.
    (different)

—"My November Guest" (1913)

QUESTIONS SECTION

O Romeo, Romeo! Wherefore art thou Romeo?

—William Shakespeare, *Romeo and Juliet* (1597)

The Rule of Three: Questions*

(1) **Children:** The Rule of Three gets ingrained early in life. Complete these phrases, all of which come from material designed for children of various ages.

- C. S. Lewis: *The Lion, the Witch, and the* _____
- *The Little Engine That Could*: "I think I can. I think I can. _____."
- *Superman*: "It's a bird. It's a _____. It's Superman!"
- The Big Bad Wolf: "I'll huff, and I'll puff, and I'll _____."

(2) **Slogans:** Nonprofit organizations often have the Rule of Three in their slogans. Match the slogan with the organization that has used it.

Slogan	Organization
"Defending. Empowering. Influencing."	Habitat for Humanitiy
"We build strenght, stability, and self-reliance through shelter."	American Civil Liberties Union (ACLU)
"Helping youth is a key to building a more conscientious, responsible, and productive society."	Boy Scouts of America

---

* For answers, see page 221 of Appendix C.

(3) **Alliteration:** The Rule of Three is often combined with alliteration. Fill in the blank in the sentences below. Even if you don't
recognize the sentence, you may be able to figure out the missing
word, given that it starts with the same letter as the other items
in the list.

> "It is not from the benevolence of the butcher, the brewer,
> or the _____ that we expect our dinner, but from their
> regard to their own interest."
> > —Adam Smith, *The Wealth of Nations* (1776)

> "In subsequent cases also, we have recognized the
> fundamental right of parents to make decisions concerning
> the _____, custody, and control of their children."
> > —Justice Sandra Day O'Connor, *Troxel v. Granville* (2000)

> "We are a free clinic staffed by Michigan Law students that
> provides Unemployment Insurance advocacy, _____, and
> assistance to Michigan workers."
> > —website of the Unemployment Insurance Clinic
> > at the University of Michigan Law School

(4) **Titles:** The titles of books and articles often use the Rule of Three. From the two lists below, match the title with the subtitle.

Title
- *Lean In* by Sheryl Sandberg
- *Nudge* by Cass Sunstein and Richard Thaler
- *Superfreakonomics* by Steven Levitt and Stephen Dubner
- *The Bully Pulpit* by Doris Kearns Goodwin

Subtitle
- *Improving Decisions About Health, Wealth, and Happiness*
- *Women, Work, and the Will to Lead*
- *Theodore Roosevelt, William Howard Taft, and the Golden Age of Journalism*
- *Global Cooling, Patriotic Prostitutes, and Why Suicide Bombers Should Buy Life Insurance*

(5) **Ugly Side:** I often tell my students that there is an ugly side to the Rule of Three, by which I mean that the Rule of Three's attractive rhythm has been used to promote some unattractive causes. Match the offensive phrases below with their original source.

Phrase
- "Segregation now. Segregation tomorrow. Segregation forever!"
- "Gas, Grass, or Ass. Nobody rides for free."
- "Remember the weak, meek, and ignorant are always good targets."
- "We can delay and effectively stop for a temporary period of indefinite length the number of immigrants into the United States. We could do this by simply advising our consuls to put every obstacle in the way and to require additional evidence and to resort to various administrative devices which would <u>postpone</u> and <u>postpone</u> and <u>postpone</u> the granting of the visas."
- "Ein Volk, Ein Reich, Ein Führer." (Translation: "One People, One Nation, One Leader.")

Source
- slogan of Adolf Hitler and the Nazi Party
- former governor of Alabama George Wallace
- bumper sticker targeted by anti–human trafficking groups
- memo given to unscrupulous bond sellers who would eventually be implicated in the 1980s Savings and Loans Crisis
- memo written by State Department official Breckinridge Long about how to avoid offering visas to Jewish refugees during World War II

EXAMPLES SECTION

Here are the two best prayers I know: "Help me, help me, help me," and "Thank you, thank you, thank you."

—Anne Lamott, *Travelling Mercies: Some Thoughts on Faith* (1999)

The Rule of Three: Examples

(1) **History:** "The boy should read history, the first John Adams wrote to his wife, Abigail, about the education of their son, John Quincy. History. History. History."

—David McCullough, *Brave Companions: Portraits in History* (1991)

(2) **Globalization:** "It happened when we connected New York, New Mexico, and California. It happened when we connected Western Europe, America, and Japan. And it will happen when we connect India and China with America, Europe, and Japan. The way to succeed is not by stopping the railroad line from connecting you, but by upgrading your skills and making the investment in those practices that will enable you and your society to claim your slice of the bigger but more complex pie."

—Thomas Friedman, *The World Is Flat* (2005)

(3) **Sylvia Plath:** "I took a deep breath and listened to the old brag of my heart. I am, I am, I am."

—Sylvia Plath, *The Bell Jar* (1963)

(4) **Kevin Young:** "We breathe, / we grieve, we drink / our tidy drinks."

—Kevin Young, "Money Road" (2016)

(5) **Angela Duckworth:** "Instead of pumps, pearls, and a tailored suit, I wore sensible shoes I could stand in all day and dresses I wouldn't mind getting covered in chalk."

—Angela Duckworth, *Grit: The Power of Passion and Perseverance* (2016)

(6) **Guy Fawkes Day:** "Remember, remember, the fifth of November. Gunpowder, treason, and plot."

—English folk verse

(7) **Trial Courts:** "The cornerstone of the American judicial system is the trial courts . . . in which witnesses testify, juries deliberate, and justice is done."

—Justice William Rehnquist, engraving in the Lloyd George Federal Courthouse in Las Vegas, Nevada

(8) **T. S. Eliot:** "Shantih shantih shantih."

—T. S. Eliot, final words of "The Waste Land" (1922)

PRACTICE SECTION

Faster, Higher, Stronger.

—Olympic motto

Practice Section: Notes on Nuance

Background

The Rule of Three gives you an opportunity to enhance the way you use

- the preposition "to"
- coordinating conjunctions*

Becoming skilled with both will help add nuance to the way you communicate. You'll discover new rhythms and pairings, each of which will help you better organize and express your ideas and observations. You'll also start to learn the hidden mechanics behind what makes people good with words. The secret is not effortless inspiration. The secret is a kind of disciplined imitation that moves from understanding, to mastery, to innovation. Said differently, in Rule of Three structure:

Learn the form.
Master the form.
And then make the form your own.

---

* Coordinating conjunctions are words like "and," "or," and "nor" that bring together—or "conjoin"—different parts of a sentence.

Assignment

Read the following two sections of "Notes on Nuance." Then try to imitate the examples.

For the examples involving the preposition "to," imitate them by revising a sentence you have written to help advance your academic or professional career. Good places to look include:

- your résumé
- your LinkedIn profile
- a cover letter you recently wrote
- an application essay you recently wrote
- any other kind of document or website that has biographical information about you

You don't have to stick with the revision. I just want you to practice the technique and see that with anything you write, you have compositional options.

For the examples using coordinating conjunctions, revise a sentence in which you have told a story or narrated a set of facts about someone other than yourself. Good places to look include:

- a legal brief
- an academic essay
- a recommendation letter
- a mission statement
- an annual report
- a review of a restaurant, movie, song, book, exhibition, store, event, or anything else you can think of

Again, you don't have to stick with the revision. The point is to experiment with writing moves you might not have known about—or at least become more conscious of and deliberate with ones you may already be using.

Notes on Nuance: "To"

1. Note how "to" is used to cover and connect a large range of material.

Willie Wonka: "If these fates seem a little gruesome to you, reflect that all great children's tales are a little gruesome, from *The Brothers Grimm* to *Alice in Wonderland* to *Snow White*, and certainly not excluding *Mother Goose*."

—Roger Ebert, movie review of
Willy Wonka and the Chocolate Factory (1971)

Pablo Neruda: "A friend told me to take along some Neruda, and I have ever since, that same weathered book always in the top of my tattered green pack, from Cuba to Mexico to the silver stones of Macchu Picchu."

—Mark Eisner, introduction to
The Essential Neruda: Selected Poems (2004)

2. Note how "to" is often combined with alliteration.

Jewish Justices: "From Benjamin to Brandeis to Breyer: Is There a Jewish Seat on the United States Supreme Court?"

—title of speech by
Justice Ruth Bader Ginsburg (2003)

Hollister: "Fifteen years ago, the word 'Hollister' meant little to anyone. Now it's hard to walk around any city, from Melbourne to Montreal to Mumbai, without seeing it stitched on someone's shirt or hoodie."

—Dave Eggers, "The Actual Hollister" (2015)

3. Note how "to" sometimes appears with commas and sometimes doesn't. The difference seems to be how fast you want the reader to get through the list.

Green Card Application: "The danger could range from making her work for him, to beating her up, to making her disappear."
—student at the University of Michigan Law School representing a client in the Human Trafficking Clinic (2016)

Katharine Hepburn: "There you were—really the greatest movie actor. I say this because I believe it and also I have heard many people of standing in your business say it. From Oliver to Lee Strasberg to David Lean. You name it. You could do it."
—Katharine Hepburn, letter to her husband, Spencer Tracy, twenty years after his death (1991)

4. Note how "to" works well in online bios and similar descriptions of experience and expertise.

Supreme Court Superstar: "He has argued 32 cases in the [Supreme] Court, on issues ranging from criminal procedure to maritime law to civil and human rights."
—faculty bio of Professor Jeff Fisher, the codirector of the Supreme Court Litigation Clinic at Stanford Law School and a graduate of the University of Michigan Law School (2017)

Résumé: "Handled all aspects of the appeal, from client counseling to writing the brief to doing oral argument."
—résumé of University of Michigan student (2017)

5. Note how "to" is often combined with the Rule of Three.

Child Custody: "She warns clients that everything they do could be brought into court, from their emails <u>to</u> their antidepressant prescriptions <u>to</u> the case of wine they bought online for a party."

—Susanna Schrobsdorff, "Divorce: The New Rules of Child Custody" (2008)

6. Note how "to" doesn't have to be combined with the Rule of Three. Sometimes "to" just connects two items and starts with "from."

Barbie: "It is difficult to imagine that the Barbie Doll, so perfect in her sculpture and presentation, and so comfortable in every setting, <u>from</u> California girl <u>to</u> Chief Executive Officer Barbie, could spawn such acrimonious litigation and such egregious conduct on the part of the challenger."

—Judge M. Margaret McKeown, *Christian v. Mattel* (2002)

Iron Curtain: "<u>From</u> Stettin in the Baltic <u>to</u> Trieste in the Adriatic, an iron curtain has descended across the continent."

—Winston Churchill, "Iron Curtain" speech (1946)

7. Note how "to" can also connect more than two or three items.

Neural Firing: "The implications of writing signals into the brain, or neuromodulation, however, were far more wide-reaching than that: being able to control neural firing would conceivably allow treatment of a host of currently untreatable or intractable neurological and psychiatric diseases, from

70

major depression <u>to</u> Huntington's <u>to</u> schizophrenia <u>to</u>
Tourette's <u>to</u> OCD—the possibilities were limitless."
—Paul Kalanithi, *When Breath Becomes Air* (2016)

Notes on Nuance: Adding Coordinating Conjunctions

1. Note how adding an extra conjunction to a list of three items can give the list a boost of energy and speed. Momentum builds. Information accumulates.

George Bernard Shaw: "Remember that you are a human being with a soul and the divine gift of articulate speech: that your native language is the language of Shakespeare <u>and</u> Milton <u>and</u> The Bible."
—George Bernard Shaw, *Pygmalion* (1916)

Sandra Day O'Connor: "Like the prudential component, the constitutional component of standing doctrine incorporates concepts concededly not susceptible of precise definition. The injury alleged must be, for example, 'distinct and palpable,' and not 'abstract' <u>or</u> 'conjectural' <u>or</u> 'hypothetical.'"
—Justice Sandra Day O'Connor, *Allen v. Wright* (1984)

2. Note how the individual items in the list can be longer than just a word or two.

Little Green Men: "The sole exception to this rule lies with allegations that are sufficiently fantastic to defy reality as we know it: claims about little green men, <u>or</u> the plaintiff's recent trip to Pluto, <u>or</u> experiences in time travel. That is not what we have here."
—Justice David Souter, *Ashcroft v. Iqbal* (2008)

Second Amendment: "The Court's opinion should not be taken to cast doubt on longstanding prohibitions on the possession of firearms by felons and the mentally ill, <u>or</u> laws forbidding the carrying of firearms in sensitive places such as schools and government buildings, <u>or</u> laws imposing conditions and qualifications on the commercial sale of arms."
—Justice Antonin Scalia, *District of Columbia v. Heller* (2008)

3. Note how the list doesn't have to include three items. It can include many more than that.

John Updike: "They shopped, <u>and</u> saw, <u>and</u> slept, <u>and</u> ate."
—John Updike, *Too Far to Go: The Maple Stories* (1979)

Jill Lepore: "The upstarts who work at startups don't often stay at any one place for very long. (Three out of four startups fail. More than nine out of ten never earn a return.) They work a year here, a few months there—zany hours everywhere. They wear jeans <u>and</u> sneakers <u>and</u> ride scooters <u>and</u> share offices <u>and</u> sprawl on couches like Great Danes. Their coffee machines look like dollhouse-size factories."
—Jill Lepore, "The Disruption Machine" (2014)

4. Note how the list might just be the same word over and over and over again.

Evicted: "She dialed a number. Her cousin who owed her didn't pick up. She dialed a number. Her foster care mother said her house was full. She dialed a number. She dialed <u>and</u> dialed <u>and</u> dialed <u>and</u> dialed."
—Matthew Desmond, *Evicted: Poverty and Profit in the American City* (2016)

72

The Big Short: "In the five years since he had started, the S&P 500, against which he was measured, was down 6.84 percent. In the same period, he reminded his investors, Scion Capital was up 242 percent. He assumed he'd earned the rope to hang himself. He assumed wrong. 'I'm building breathtaking sand castles,' he wrote, 'but nothing stops the tide from coming <u>and</u> coming <u>and</u> coming.'"
—Michael Lewis, The Big Short (2010)

5. Note how "and" and "or" tend to be used the most—but you can also use "nor."

Dover Beach: *"Ah, love, let us be true*
> *To one another! for the world, which seems*
> *To lie before us like a land of dreams,*
> *So various, so beautiful, so new,*
> *Hath really neither joy, <u>nor</u> love, <u>nor</u> light,*
> *<u>Nor</u> certitude, <u>nor</u> peace, <u>nor</u> help for pain."*

—Matthew Arnold, "Dover Beach" (1867)

The technical name for adding extra conjunctions is "polysyndeton":

poly ("many") + **syndeton** ("conjunction") = **polysyndeton**

But when I first used the term with a class of University of Michigan undergraduates, they told me that "polysyndeton" was too hard to remember, that it is sounded like some strange chemical compound—the kind of thing you might use to insulate your attic.

So we created a different term, one that pays homage to Neil Gaiman, a writer who uses polysyndeton often and well. We called it the "Gaiman Grab," because the move helps you grab more and more material into your sentences.

Gaiman writes science fiction novels. But he also writes children's stories and screenplays and graphic novels and a whole bunch of other stuff. Which is why he seemed like an appropriate ambassador for polysyndeton: his writing embodies a similar kind of hyperinclusion.

Here, for example, is a cheerfully overpacked New Year's wish Gaiman first posted on his website in 2001. (He has pledged to repost it every three years.):

> May your coming year be filled with magic <u>and</u> dreams <u>and</u> good madness. I hope you read some fine books and kiss someone who thinks you're wonderful, and don't forget to make some art—write <u>or</u> draw <u>or</u> build <u>or</u> sing <u>or</u> live only as you can.

And here is a line from *Make Good Art*, a book based on a commencement speech he gave at the University of the Arts in 2012:

> I wanted to write comic books <u>and</u> novels <u>and</u> stories <u>and</u> films.

You obviously don't have to adopt the term "Gaiman Grab" to use and master polysyndeton. If you prefer and can more easily remember the technical term, stick with that. My undergraduates and I were just searching for a something a little more catchy.

* * *

That same rationale led us to come up with the term "Touch of Twain" for "asyndeton," which is polysyndeton's rhetorical counterpart: instead of adding conjunctions, asyndeton takes them away.

The disclaimer Mark Twain puts at the beginning of *The Adventures of Huckleberry Finn* is a good example. He could have written it this way:

> Persons attempting to find a motive in this narrative will be prosecuted; persons attempting to find a moral in it will be banished; <u>and</u> persons attempting to find a plot in it will be shot.

But instead he took out the conjunction:

> Persons attempting to find a motive in this narrative will be prosecuted; persons attempting to find a moral in it will be banished; persons attempting to find a plot in it will be shot.

The result is a sentence that is a bit more sleek and dramatic. The rhythm is different. The shape is different. The absent conjunction is not missed one bit.

The same is true in the sentence below, from a letter Twain wrote to the editor of the *Atlantic Monthly*, William Dean Howells, in 1878. Twain is complaining about a recent trip to Germany:

> Munich did seem the horriblest place, the most desolate place, the most unendurable place!

The lack of a conjunction isn't accidental. Twain didn't commit a typo. He clearly wanted his words to have a certain rhythm and shape, as did Abraham Lincoln when he described, in the Gettysburg Address, a "government of the people, by the people, for the people." But a "Touch of Lincoln" doesn't have quite the same ring to it as a "Touch of Twain," so we went with Twain.

You, however, are welcome to call asyndeton anything you want. Choose whatever works best for your brain.

FOUR

Sound and Sense

This is what I mean when I call myself a writer. I construct sentences. There's a rhythm I hear that drives me through a sentence.

—Don DeLillo, "Don DeLillo: The Art of Fiction No. 135" (1993)

Sound and Sense: Concept

"My calculation is [Justice Antonin Scalia and I] spent about eighty-five to one hundred hours side by side [working on our book]," [Bryan] Garner said. "Probably sixty of those hours, once we had a draft, we actually went through sentence by sentence, together, reading it aloud."

—Alex Carp, "Writing with Antonin Scalia, Grammar Nerd" (2012)

There is a special relationship between sound and sense. What helps improve the sound of a sentence usually helps improve the sense of that sentence, by which I mean its clarity and content. Similarly, what helps improve the sense of a sentence usually helps improve the sound. The two qualities are nicely symbiotic.

The poet Alexander Pope articulated the connection between sound and sense back in 1711. In the lyrical lines of "An Essay on Criticism," he suggests that it is not enough that the sound of a poem not "give offense." To be a really exceptional piece of verse, the sound must link up with the meaning of words as well. "The sound," he writes, "must seem an echo to the sense."

Robert Frost made a similar suggestion in a letter to a former student in 1913. Frost explained that it is possible to have sense without sound and that it is possible to have sound without sense—but the real goal is to construct sentences that merge sound and sense together. Good sound isn't enough. Good sense isn't enough. A deliberate combination is needed. Frost even goes so far as to insist that "an ear and an appetite for these sounds of sense is the first qualification of a writer, be it of prose or verse."

The endorsement of a final writer, Joan Didion, cements the point. In "Why I Write," which is the essay we looked at in chapter 2 when introducing "the infinite power of grammar," Didion highlights the importance she places not just on the meaning of words—not just on their "sense"—but also on their "sound," on the music they make when arranged in sequence. Here is how the essay begins:

Of course I stole the title for this essay from George Orwell.

Didion is referring to an essay with the same title ("Why I Write") that George Orwell published in 1946. Her discussion of sound comes next:

> One reason I stole [the title] was that I like the sound of the words. Why I Write. There you have three short unambiguous words that share a sound, and the sound they share is this: I, I, I.

She then connects this sound to what she considers one of the main goals of writing—she connects sound to sense: "In many ways writing is the act of saying *I*, of imposing oneself upon other people, of saying *listen to me, see it my way, change your mind*. It is an aggressive, even a hostile act." Later in the essay, she offers a tidy way to think about this link between meaning and music, between the mechanics of writing and the melody words can produce: "Grammar is a piano I play by ear."

Grammar as an instrument, as something you can master and enjoy without much formal training: that seems like a much better approach to writing than some boring lesson on parts of speech.

Meaning and Rhythm

Didion herself apparently began this approach at a very young age. In *The Year of Magical Thinking*, her 2005 account of the twelve months following the death of her husband, John Dunne, she recounts how she discovered the interaction of sound and sense: "As a writer, even as a child, long before what I wrote began to be published, I developed a sense that meaning itself was resident in the rhythms of words and sentences and paragraphs."

Didion is making essentially the same point as Pope and Frost. She is saying that sound and sense go together, that they are intertwined and mutually beneficial. When you add some sound to a sentence, the sense gets better; when you add some sense, the sound gets better. Each enhances the power and effect of the other.

Which is why perhaps the best way to edit a piece of writing is to read it aloud. Or even better, have somebody else read it out loud to you. Many errors slip past your eyes, especially if you make the mistake of trying to edit on a computer screen. Fewer slip past your ears. This difference is even more pronounced if you print out what you have written, go to some place different from where you drafted it, and then ask another person to help you hear the words—not as you think you composed them, but as they actually appear on the page.

It's like what the world-class violinist Itzhak Perlman does to improve the way his playing sounds to audiences: he gets an extra ear.

Extra Ear

A description of what Perlman means by an "extra ear" appears in the essay "Personal Best" by the writer and surgeon Atul Gawande. The essay examines how improvement happens and how plateauing—at your job, at a certain skill, at your favorite hobby or sport—can be prevented, or at least curtailed.

Perlman is one of a number of elite musicians Gawande interviewed. Another is the opera soprano Renée Fleming, who has been invited to perform at such prestigious venues as the White House, the Supreme Court, Buckingham Palace, the 20th anniversary of the Czech Republic's "Velvet Revolution," the Nobel Peace Prize ceremony, and the Super Bowl. Both Perlman and Fleming swear by extra ears, which are simply people you trust to give you candid, constructive feedback on how you sound.

"The great challenge in performing is listening to yourself," Perlman told Gawande. "Your physicality, the sensation that you have as you play the violin, interferes with your accuracy of listening." Perlman therefore considers himself lucky to receive constant coaching from his wife, Toby, a concert-level violinist he met at music camp more than 50 years ago. Toby has been Perlman's extra ear ever since. "She'd tell him if a passage was too fast or too tight or too mechanical," Gawande explains. "Her ear provides external judgment."

Fleming uses a slightly different term to describe her extra ears—she calls them her "outside ears." But she finds them no less essential. Her reason? "What we hear as we are singing is not what the audience hears." The extra ear fills that divide.

A similar thing can be said of writing: what we hear as we are writing is not what the reader hears. There is often a gap between intention and effect, between what you plan to write and what you actually produce. Without someone to fill that gap, without an extra ear, our writing risks being confusing, awkward, dull, repetitive, incomplete—the worst kind of music.

The Trouble with Intentions

Verlyn Klinkenborg knows this gap well. A longtime teacher of writing and a former member of the *New York Times* editorial board, he understands that "on their own, sentences are implacably honest."

In a 2012 essay called "The Trouble with Intentions," he observes that sentences "may be long, short, simple, complex, clear, ambiguous, even incoherent. But they don't try to hide those qualities. They are what they are and they say what they say." The problem is that writers aren't always able to see these qualities, particularly when the qualities are negative. Klinkenborg has looked at countless sentences that are deficient in various ways—they're cumbersome, redundant, jumbled, contradictory—and he has asked himself: Why didn't the writers catch these mistakes? Why couldn't they see the obvious flaws the reader now has to suffer through?

His answer: "The sentence, as written, was invisible to them."

Getting an extra ear—or, if you prefer, an extra eye—is the single best way I know to address this problem. I have been doing it with my own students for more than a decade. Every time they submit a legal brief or academic essay, every time they put together a memo or résumé, I encourage them to get an "extra ear" before sending it off.

When I teach undergraduate courses, I actually make the students identify their extra ear at the bottom of the last page of each paper they hand in. The extra ear can be their roommate. It can be a classmate. It can be a friend or parent or sibling. It can be just about anyone—as long as it is not them.

My favorite example came in the fall of 2012, when I was teaching a course called "The Syntax of Sports." A first-year student wrote a wonderful essay about the Detroit Tigers that I could tell had been helpfully revised several times. The following words appeared at the bottom of the last page, with what seemed like a not insubstantial amount of pride:

Extra Ear: Jerry Halperin (my grandpa)

It ended up being the best essay in the class.

Chief Justice John Roberts

Chief Justice John Roberts used extra ears all the time when he was an appellate lawyer at the law firm now known as Hogan Lovells. The advice he gives about this habit, in an interview published in the *Scribes Journal of Legal Writing*, is worth quoting at length:

> Before the brief is due or filed, in a little bit of time and comfortably before the argument, sit down with either a layperson or a colleague in your firm or office that has nothing to do with the case. A non-litigator is what I look for. And just drop the brief on them and say, "Look, can you spend a half hour—and read this brief and tell me what you think?"
>
> He'll look at it and say, "This is an ERISA preemption case. I don't know anything about that."
>
> And you say, "Just read."

If that person can't come back to you after reading through it once and answer these two questions—(1) what is this case about? (2) why should I win?—you need to go back and start over.

You don't need to be working on a legal brief to try this technique out. A perfectly sensible thing to ask someone you show, say, a cover letter is: "Would you please read this and then tell me two things: (1) What is this cover letter about? (2) Why should the organization hire me?" Other variations exist:

Application Essay: (1) What is this application essay about? (2) Why should the school accept me?

Contract: (1) What is this contract about? (2) Why should both parties sign it?

Grant Proposal: (1) What is this grant about? (2) Why should the donor fund it?

Client Pitch: (1) What is this pitch about? (2) Why should the client go for it?

Apology: (1) What is the apology about? (2) Why should the person forgive me?

The questions sound simple. But it's amazing how often an extra ear will not be able to answer them. Not because the extra ear is a dullard. That's rarely the case. More frequently, the extra ear will not be able to answer these questions because the writer, so wrapped up in her own thinking, will not have clearly included the answers in the document. Don't make that mistake. Before handing any assignment in—or certainly before filing or publishing any document—make sure at least one other set of eyes reads it over. Your set is not to be trusted.

Another way to think about this point is to realize that writing often comes down to having a conversation on the page—only first, that conversation needs to happen with another person. So talk to people about what you are writing. Listen to their feedback. Incorporate what you find helpful. Ignore what you don't. And then thank them profusely.

Chances are, their input will help you improve what you eventually produce—both in terms of its sound and its sense.

QUESTIONS SECTION

I used to hate it when a book came out or a story was published and I would be like "Damn, how did I not catch that [mistake]?" But you pretty much always catch it when you're reading out loud.

—David Sedaris, quoted by Kristin Hohenadel in "Say It Out Loud: How David Sedaris Makes His Writing Better" (2013)

Sound and Sense: Questions*

(1) **Film:** In 1982, the film critic Charlie Champlin described the genius of Alfred Hitchcock movies this way: "The Hitchcock touch has four hands." Two of these hands, Champlin said, belonged to Hitchcock himself. The other two belonged to what we might call Hitchcock's "extra ear"—the person who read every script, watched every scene, and continually offered the kind of candid feedback nobody else could get away with. Once, in response to this person's observation that "You might not be the easiest man to live with, but you do know how to cut a picture better than anybody else," Hitchcock apparently responded, with great admiration, "Except for you."

Identify the person.
(A) Alma Reville (Hitchcock's wife)
(B) William Hitchcock (Hitchcock's father)
(C) Emma Jean Hitchcock (Hitchcock's mother)
(D) Orson Welles
(E) François Truffaut

---

* For answers, see page 224 of Appendix C.

(2) **Supreme Court:** One of the justices on the Supreme Court claims to have learned the most about writing from two people: the first is the justice's mother, the second is the justice's former thesis adviser at Princeton. Here is an appreciative description of the extra-ear-like role the thesis adviser played:

> Princeton demands a very lengthy kind of project in your last year of college. It was 100 pages—150 pages, or something like that—and Sean Wilentz, my adviser, must have read every sentence of it at least three times, in different drafts, constantly critiquing my work and my writing. That experience was probably the first time in my life when somebody who himself was a fabulous writer spent so much time, sentence by sentence, telling me what I could do better.

Identify the justice.
(A) Justice Neil Gorsuch
(B) Justice Samuel Alito
(C) Justice Sonia Sotomayor
(D) Justice Clarence Thomas
(E) Justice Elena Kagan

(3) **Novels:** Some of the world's most well-known novels started out with different titles. Only after the intervention of an extra ear (or several) was a change made. Match the published version of the title with its earlier draft.

Final Version	*Earlier Draft*
To Kill a Mockingbird	"The War of the Ring"
The Lord of the Rings	"The Last Man in Europe"
Catch-22	"Twilight"
Pride and Prejudice	"Atticus"
Dracula	"The Dead Un-Dead"
War and Peace	"All's Well That Ends Well"
1984	"First Impressions"
The Sound and the Fury	"Catch-11"
The Grapes of Wrath	"Strangers From Within"
The Lord of the Flies	"Trimalchio in West Egg"
The Great Gatsby	"The Great Pig Sticking"

(4) **Stand-Up Comedy:** In her memoir *The Girl with the Lower Back Tattoo*, the comedian Amy Schumer describes the wonderful extra ear a fellow comedian provided for her as she worked to improve some of her stage material: "One night we talked after we'd both performed on Night of Too Many Stars, an event to raise money for autism. My set had been strong, and _____ stopped by the greenroom and offered to help me if I ever needed it. Which sounds creepy, but it's not. He said exactly what he meant. When you have the disease of being a comic, and you see someone else with some talent and respect for comedy, you want to help. It's in his veins. It's in my veins. A little later, I called his bluff, which was anything but. He started riding around and going to clubs with me to watch my set, give me notes, and help me get better."

Identify the comedian who helped Schumer. Part of his name has already been filled in below.

First Name: C _ _ _S
Last Name: _ _ C K

(5) **Pixar:** In *Creativity, Inc.*, Ed Catmull describes a kind of Group Extra Ear he helped develop as one of the cofounders of Pixar. Called "the Braintrust," the group provides the company's film directors with helpful feedback on early drafts of their current project. Here are what Catmull sees as the Braintrust's two defining characteristics:

> The first is that the Braintrust is made up of people with a deep understanding of storytelling, who usually have been through the process themselves. While the directors welcome critiques from many sources, they particularly prize feedback from fellow storytellers. The second difference is that the Braintrust has no authority. The director does not have to follow any of the specific suggestions. After a Braintrust meeting, it is up to him or her to figure out how to address the feedback. Giving the Braintrust no power to mandate solutions affects the dynamics of the group in ways I believe are essential.

What would a Braintrust look like at your organization? Who would you want in it?

For some helpful advice on the second question ("Who would you want in your Braintrust?") consider the approach of Andrew Stanton, one of the original members of the Braintrust at Pixar and the writer or director (and sometimes both) of *Toy Story*, *Finding Nemo*, *A Bug's Life*, *Monsters Inc.*, and *WALL-E*:

> Here are the qualifications [I look for]: The people you choose must (a) make you think smarter and (b) put lots of solutions on the table in a short amount of time. I don't care who it is, the janitor or the intern or one of your most-trusted lieutenants: If they can help you do that, they should be at the table.

EXAMPLES SECTION

I always, ALWAYS, read my work out loud as I'm writing. It's the single best tool for self-editing.

—Susan Orlean, Twitter (2012)

Sound and Sense: Examples

(1) **Copyediting:** "The whole point of having things read before publication is to test their effect on a general reader. You want to make sure when you go out there that the tag on the back of the collar isn't poking up—unless, of course, you are deliberately wearing your clothes inside out."

—Mary Norris, *Between You & Me: Confessions of a Comma Queen* (2016)

(2) **Oliver Sacks:** "[My editor] Colin had to pick among many versions, restrain my sometimes overabundant prose, and create a continuity. Sometimes he would say, pointing to one passage, 'This doesn't go here,' then flip the pages over, saying, 'It goes *here.*' As soon as he said this, I would see he was right, but—mysteriously—I could not see it for myself."

—Oliver Sacks, *On the Move: A Life* (2015)

(3) **Judge Learned Hand:** "In writing his memos and opinions, [Judge Learned] Hand worked with a legal-size pad of yellow paper, which he propped on a board resting on his knees or set on his desk. Before getting down a word, he would tell [his law clerk] what he planned to write in, say, the first two paragraphs, and then invite—indeed, press—him to offer criticisms. Hand took these [criticisms] very seriously. The clerk would then return to his

own desk while Hand wrote out the first paragraph in longhand. Soon, Hand would give the yellow sheets to the clerk for renewed criticism; if the clerk had objections and Hand saw merit in them, he would try again. He repeated that procedure for page after long yellow page of his drafts, continuing to press for comment; in the most difficult cases, he would go through as many as thirteen draft opinions with many crossings-out and much rewriting before he permitted his secretary to prepare a typewritten version and distribute it to his fellow judges."

—Gerald Gunther, *Learned Hand: The Man and the Judge* (1994)

(4) **Breaking Bad:** "Studios and networks have a reputation for diluting the creative process with their notes. Decision by committee. Conservatism rules. But extra eyes on a story line can actually be useful and generative, and throughout the run of *Breaking Bad* our studio and our network helped make the story better."

—Bryan Cranston, *A Life in Parts* (2016)

(5) **Francine Prose:** "Read your work aloud, if you can, if you aren't too embarrassed by the sound of your voice ringing out when you are alone in a room. Chances are that the sentence you can hardly pronounce without stumbling is a sentence that needs to be reworked to make it smoother and more fluent. A poet once told me that he was reading a draft of a new poem aloud to himself when a thief broke into his Manhattan loft. Instantly surmising that he had entered the dwelling of a madman, the thief turned and ran without taking anything, and without harming the poet. So it may be that reading your work aloud will not only improve its quality but save your life in the process."

—Francine Prose, *Reading Like a Writer: A Guide for People Who Love Books and for Those Who Want to Write Them* (2006)

(6) **Albert Einstein:** "In addition, he produced an even more understandable version: a book for the lay reader, *Relativity: The Special and the General Theory*, that remains popular to this day. To make sure that the average person would fathom it, he read every page aloud to Elsa's daughter Margot, pausing frequently to ask whether she indeed got it."

—Walter Isaacson, *Einstein: His Life and Universe* (2007)

(7) **Business Letters:** "The acid test—read your letter out loud when you're done. You might get a shock—but you'll know for sure if it sounds natural."

—Malcolm Forbes (longtime publisher of *Forbes*), "How to Write a Business Letter" (1985)

(8) **Lawyers:** "We've already talked about the value of reciting your prose as you create to capture the right feel. It's even more important to do the same thing when you edit your writing. First, doing so slows you down so you can capture mistakes more easily. More important, prose that doesn't sound like something you would say . . . is something you likely shouldn't write either. That's why novelists such as John Irving read their work aloud before publishing."

—Steven Stark, *Writing to Win: The Legal Writer* (2012)

PRACTICE SECTION

[Gustave Flaubert] considered the more subtle rhymes and rhythms of prose to be of supreme importance; therefore he often tested his drafts by reading them to himself or to his friends out loud, at times raising his voice to an enthusiastic shout.
—Laurence Porter, *A Gustave Flaubert Encyclopedia* (2001)

Practice Section #1: Record and Revise

Background

If you can't find somebody to be your extra ear or you are not yet comfortable sharing your draft with another person, technology can help. Most computers and smartphones allow you to record the sound of your voice. So take something you've written and read it into the recorder, or at least read part of it. Even doing this with a single paragraph can help.

Assignment

Once you have finished the recording, don't listen to it immediately. Give yourself an hour, an afternoon, or even better, a whole day or week to get some editorial distance. You'll hear your words in a new way the longer you spend away from them.

When you finally do decide to listen, make sure you have a pen and paper handy so that you can jot down notes to the following questions:

- What problem spots do I hear?
- Where are the transitions not tight enough?
- Where are the details not compelling enough?
- Where are there words that can be cut?
- Where are there words that need to be added?
- What section or sentence can the reader point to and say, "OK, here is where I learned something important"?

There are other questions you can ask as well, questions about organization, about themes, about originality and style. But these should give you a good start. The point is to start to approach your writing as what the novelist Zadie Smith calls "a smart stranger."

Additional Note: Everybody I have ever asked to do this exercise has reported that (1) it is painful and (2) it is *super* helpful. The pain tends to diminish the more you do the exercise. The super helpfulness, fortunately, often goes in the opposite direction: the first time you listen to a recording of yourself, you'll probably cringe, like that awkward experience of hearing a message you left on somebody else's voice mail. But soon you'll get used to it and be able to better focus not on the sound of your vocals but on the rhythm of your words. A lot of editing involves tinkering with that rhythm.

Practice Section #2: Record and Compare

Background

Take an article from a well-edited magazine or newspaper. If you are into business and politics, try the *Economist* or the *Wall Street Journal*. If you are into food, try a restaurant review in the *Los Angeles Times*, *Washington Post*, or *Times-Picayune* (in New Orleans). Or maybe your preference leans more toward short fiction, in which case publications like *Granta*, *Tinhouse*, and *McSweeney's* all have great offerings, as do designated sections of *Harper's*, *Ploughshares*, and the *New Yorker*. This list is not at all exhaustive. There is plenty of great writing only a newsstand or a few mouse clicks away.

Assignment

The point is to record yourself reading the work of highly skilled writers and editors. You don't have to read the whole piece. A page or two will suffice. Just make sure you go slowly and try to follow the rhythm created by the words, punctuation, and paragraph breaks. Then record yourself reading something you've written recently. Finally, listen to both recordings and compare what you hear.

This comparison is unlikely to be flattering. But it will be instructive. Focus in particular on some of these potential differences:

- How does the length of the sentences compare?
- How does the variety of the sentences compare?
- How about the number and vividness of the details?
- Are there good bits of dialogue in one but not the other?
- Can you hear where there are paragraph breaks?
- Can you identify some of the themes in one more easily than you can in the other? How about the main point?

This exercise can be repeated in a more specialized, focused way. If you are a scientist, compare the sound of a paper you have written to one that has recently appeared in *Science*, *Nature*, or some other top journal. If you are a lawyer, do something similar with a brief or contract written by the best writer in your firm or organization. Even better, go talk to that person after you have done the comparison. See what they do to add sound and sense to their writing. Whatever your profession—teacher, marketer, consultant, doctor, engineer, entrepreneur, salesperson—there are probably people who have done a good job writing the kinds of things you are supposed to write. Find those people. Record yourself reading their written words. Then adjust your own approach accordingly.

Practice Section #3: Finding Your Voice(s)

Background

Think of how many emails you have sent in the past week, month, and year. Did you always strike the right tone? Did you always use the right word? Did you consistently sound the way you wanted to?

As emails are being drafted and hurriedly sent off, it is tough to stop and ask these kinds of questions, let alone answer them. But now you have the benefit of distance. So take a look at some of your archived correspondences. Read them aloud. Assess whether the voice you hear is the voice you want others to hear.

Don't expect the voice you hear to be consistent. You'd be horrible at emails if it were. As the psychologist and philosopher William James observed in his 1890 classic *The Principles of Psychology*, a person "has as many different social selves as there are distinct groups of persons about whose opinion he cares. He generally shows a different side of himself to each of these different groups. Many a youth who is demure enough before his parents and teachers, swears and swaggers like a pirate among tough friends."

This multiplicity is perhaps even more pronounced in email, a medium that allows you to craft your various "social selves" a bit more deliberately than does, say, spontaneous speech. You shouldn't email your boss or teacher the same way you email your best friend. You shouldn't email a child the same way you email an adult. And you certainly don't (I hope) email your mom the same way you email your ex.

Assignment

Focus on a small subset of the kinds of emails you send. Here are some examples:

Example Subset #1

Work

Friends

Family

Example Subset #2

Angry

Congratulatory

Appreciative

Example Subset #3

To your teachers

To prospective employers

To prospective love interests

Example Subset #4

When you've missed a deadline

When somebody else has missed a deadline

When you have requested (or granted) an extension

Pick one of these subsets, or create your own. Then read five emails from each of the categories. So if you pick Subset #1, you'd read five "Work" emails, five "Friends" emails, and five "Family" emails.

Try to find some variety within each category. If one of your "Work" emails is from last week, also read one from two or three (or more) years ago. If one of your "Friends" emails is just a few words long, also read one that spans multiple paragraphs. The idea is to get a sense of

- how you sound when writing to different people about different topics in different contexts,
- how your various voices have changed over the years,
- whether you like those changes, and
- whether you want to continue to sound as you currently do.

Your writing is empirical evidence of a lot of things: your creativity, your professionalism, your attention to detail, nuance, and context. And there is probably no larger collection of this than what exists in your email account. Even the most prolific novelists, journalists, and historians likely produce more words in email every year than they do in their published works. This is your opportunity to investigate your own written output and test whether what you've been sending out into the world matches up with the writer (and person) you want to be.

You don't need to record yourself reading any of the emails you select, but it wouldn't be the worst idea to say a few, slowly, out loud. I tell students to do that when writing very important emails. None has ever regretted taking this extra level of scrutiny. Many, however, have regretted *skipping* it, especially when they later discover a costly error, ambiguity, or bit of awkwardness.

FIVE

The Power of the Particular

If those who have studied the art of writing are in accord on any one point, it is this: the surest way to arouse and hold the reader's attention is by being specific, definite, and concrete. The greatest writers—Homer, Dante, Shakespeare— are effective largely because they deal in particulars and report the details that matter. Their words call up pictures.

—William Strunk Jr. and E. B. White,
The Elements of Style (1959)

The Power of the Particular: Concept

Without the minuteness of execution, the sublime cannot exist. Grandeur of ideas is founded on precision of ideas.

—William Blake, *William Blake's Annotations to Sir Joshua Reynolds's Discourses* (1808)

I like ideas best, as I've said, when they are most concrete.

—William Gass, *Finding a Form: Essays* (1997)

Details matter. Pick the right ones, and you can influence all kinds of decision-makers. Justice Sonia Sotomayor realized this when she was still a prosecutor in New York City back in the late 1970s and early 1980s. When crafting questions to ask witnesses at trial, she made sure to include ones that would, as she explains in her autobiography *My Beloved World*, "elicit details with powerful sensory associations—the colors, the sounds, the smells that lodge an image in the mind and put the listener in the burning house."

She treated courtroom storytelling the same way. "Before you can engage the jurors' empathy," she writes, "put them in the shoes of the accused or victim, make them feel the cold blade against their necks, or the pang of unappreciated devotion that might drive someone to steal from a former employer."

"It is the particulars," she insists, "that make a story real."

Mary Karr offers similar advice in *The Art of Memoir*, a book based on a creative writing class she teaches at Syracuse University. "A great detail," in her view, "feels particular in a way that argues for its truth." This may be why expert storytellers, legal and otherwise, seek out specific images and examples when trying to communicate their ideas. Lisa Blatt, who has argued more than 30 cases in the Supreme Court, offered the following set in her winning brief in *Adoptive Couple v. Baby Girl*, a custody battle that garnered national attention in 2013 and eventually led to Blatt's clients being reunited with the four-year-old daughter they had adopted at birth. The following quoted material is from Blatt's opening brief:

- The adoptive mother has "a Ph.D. in developmental psychology and develops therapy programs for children with behavioral problems."
- The adoptive couple had already "undergone seven unsuccessful attempts at in vitro fertilization."
- The adoptive couple was "in the delivery room during the delivery."
- The adoptive father "cut the umbilical cord."

Are any of these details legally relevant? Probably not—at least in the strictest definition of that term. The Indian Child Welfare Act, which was the governing statute in the case, says nothing about developmental psychology or therapy sessions or being "in the delivery room." Nor does any line of applicable precedent.

But that doesn't mean the details Blatt includes are not relevant in other ways. One thing they do quite well is communicate that the adoptive couple is deeply committed to becoming parents, a key factor in any custody case, regardless of the statute and precedent involved. Nobody who endures "seven unsuccessful attempts at in vitro fertilization" is still on the fence about raising a child.

The details also show that the adoptive couple has the capacity to help a child deal with the difficulties, even trauma, of enduring a multiyear lawsuit. Telling the justices that the adoptive mother has a "Ph.D. in developmental psychology" would have been good enough; adding, as Blatt does, that the adoptive mother also has experience developing "therapy programs for children with behavioral problems" is an excellent extra bit of advocacy.

Finally, the details reveal that the birth mother trusts the adoptive couple so completely that she invited them to be "in the delivery room during the delivery." The adoptive father was even the one who "cut the umbilical cord."

Justice Samuel Alito, who authored the majority opinion in the case, put special emphasis on this last detail when ruling for Blatt's clients. "Adoptive Couple was present at Baby Girl's birth in Oklahoma on September 15, 2009," he wrote, "and Adoptive Father even cut the umbilical cord." When that happens, when justices or judges pick up, indeed highlight, a compelling detail from your brief, good things usually follow. Your words, your framing, are now planted in their minds.

Sentences Nobody Else Could Write

It's not just the Supreme Court where particulars can be useful. Grants, cover letters, PowerPoint presentations, pitches to clients and boards of directors—the professional world is filled with opportunities to distinguish yourself through details. Here, for example, is a clever use of the "Interests" section on a résumé. It comes from a graduate of the University of Michigan Law School.

Interests: *Don Quixote*, Yoga, Hot Dogs

A lesser writer would have put something like this:

Interests: Reading, Exercise, Food

Or this:

Interests: Fiction, Physical Movement, Cookouts

Or maybe this:

Interests: Spanish Literature, Working Out, Grilling

What stands out about "*Don Quixote*, Yoga, Hot Dogs" is its specificity. The individualized items make it seem like the résumé was written by an actual person instead of a generic, high-achieving automaton. Plus, in a small space, you learn a lot about the applicant. You learn from *"Don Quixote"* that she is well read and possibly studied Spanish. You learn from "Yoga" that she is athletic and disciplined. And you learn from "Hot Dogs" that she has an All-American palate as well as a talent for combining unlike things together in a creative, compelling way. The juxtaposition of "Hot Dogs" with "Yoga," the immediate incongruity between those two images, has the potential to really grab a reader's attention. It's clever. It's unexpected. It may even bring a smile to the faces of members of the hiring committee—which is probably not a bad thing when trying to land an interview.

The juxtaposition is also a nice reminder that particular details have particular contexts. Not every detail plays well with others. "Hot Dogs" works well at the end of a list that already contains something intellectual (*"Don Quixote"*) and something health conscious ("Yoga"). But it might not work in every situation. You—and your words—need to be flexible.

One tactic is to use the spectrum of general-to-particular almost like you would the zoom function on Google Maps. "Here we want to zoom out for a more general, big-picture view," you might say, whether working on a contract, a mission statement, or an internal report. "But here, we want to zoom in for those nitty-gritty details."

The proper balance often involves a lot of rewriting. In December 2016, a law student asked me to help him edit an application for a fellowship he really wanted. Here is the first draft of his sentence explaining how he, a native of Russia, learned to speak English when he first came to the US in his early twenties:

I taught myself English by watching television.

That sentence is better than the even more unspecific "I taught myself English." But it is still a bit bland. So I encouraged the applicant to zoom in a little further, to add some color to the sentence, some texture, some life. I even gave him this advice: "Try to write sentences nobody else could write."

The advice is particularly well suited for application essays, personal statements, and grant proposals, where the aim is usually to tell a compelling story, to avoid clichés and platitudes, to stand out from the stack. That doesn't mean, of course, that the advice is always easy to implement. Which is why I asked the fellowship applicant some follow-up questions: What kinds of things did you watch when you were teaching yourself English? Did you have a favorite channel? A favorite show? A favorite character?

Here's what he came up with, after a couple of failed attempts:

I taught myself English by watching hours and hours of _How I Met Your Mother_.

Think of how many different ways he could have written the last part of that sentence.

I taught myself English by watching hours and hours of sitcoms.

I taught myself English by watching hours and hours of shows on CBS.

I taught myself English by watching hours and hours of a show in which a half-Jewish architect who graduated from Wesleyan University uses flashbacks to tell his children how he came to meet and marry their mother.

The first two alternatives are too general. The last is too particular. The sentence he produced beats them all. It's no longer thin and empty like "I taught myself English by watching television." It's concrete. It's personal. It's sincere. That the words didn't come to the student on his first attempt is a helpful lesson: sometimes sincerity takes a few drafts.

The Importance of a 15-Year-Old

A less dramatic but still instructive example can be seen in the editing process of another fellowship applicant. This applicant was trying to describe how the first couple of months of his Teach for America assignment at a high school in Detroit did not begin with pedagogical perfection. He included a number of good details in his initial draft, but there was still room to make his account more memorable and affecting, especially at the end of the following passage:

> The early going was rough. Within my first two months of teaching, my laptop was stolen, three separate full-on brawls broke out in my classroom, and I lost track of how many times I was cursed out.

Again, follow-up questions can be helpful. What grade did you teach? How old were the kids? What can we add to make the retelling more vivid, more real?

Remembering that the students he taught were all 15 years old seemed to do the trick. Here's the edit he happily made:

> The early going was rough. Within my first two months of teaching, my laptop was stolen, three separate full-on brawls broke out in my classroom, and I lost track of how many times I was cursed out <u>by a 15-year-old</u>.

That detail perfectly illustrates Mary Karr's point: it "feels particular in a way that argues for its truth." The same goes for the Russian applicant's detail about the television show *How I Met Your Mother* and for Lisa Blatt's details about the adoptive couple (1) enduring seven unsuccessful in vitro fertilizations, (2) being in the delivery room, and (3) even cutting the umbilical cord. They all give the sentences they appear in the stamp of credibility. They all garner trust.

Think about what it would mean if all your writing did that: if every cover letter you wrote garnered trust, if every article, email, and interoffice memo came with a stamp of credibility. Decision-makers want this kind of writing. Judges, CEOs, deans, donors—they all want to get the sense that the documents on their desks were written by someone who knows what she is talking about. They want to be confident that you are fluent in your subject matter, that you understand and can communicate the nuances of a given issue, situation, or plan.

And few things demonstrate fluency better than details.

A legal brief, for example, is nothing without convincing, evocative details. Nor is a thank-you card, restaurant review, or business plan. Good lawyers know that if you want to persuade someone to take a certain action or adopt a specific viewpoint, you'd better have something vivid and concrete to get their attention. The writer John Updike summed up this point well when he explained, back in 1985, his criteria for selecting that year's best short stories written by American authors:

"I want . . . facts . . . I can picture."

QUESTIONS SECTION

All the interesting people I know are people whose speech and thinking has a great deal of specificity to it.

—Malcolm Gladwell, "A Debate With Malcolm Gladwell," *WorkLife With Adam Grant* (2018)

The Power of the Particular: Questions*

(1) **Rolls-Royce:** A car ad from 1959 shows a picture of a shiny blue Rolls-Royce. The text of the ad, written by marketing legend David Ogilvy, contains this sentence:

> At 60 miles an hour the loudest noise in this new Rolls-Royce comes from the electric clock.

Compare that to a possible alternative sentence: "This car is really quiet."

- What's better about Ogilvy's version?
- How would you rewrite Ogilvy's version to make it too particular, the kind of thing that would clumsily overwhelm the reader with details?

---

* For answers, see page 225 of Appendix C.

(2) **A Day in the Life:** Journalists often take one or two compelling cases—such as a family, a person, or a city—and use them to comment on a much wider set of issues and events. Adrian Nicole LeBlanc does this in *Random Family*, her in-depth look at poverty in the South Bronx. Andrea Elliott does it in "Invisible Child," her multipart series for the *New York Times Magazine* on homeless children. And so does Katherine Boo in *Behind the Beautiful Forevers*, a book that focuses on an impoverished settlement in India called Annawadi to communicate a more global message.

Novelists and film directors sometimes take this technique one step further by setting a story on a single day. Match the author or film director with the single-day story they created.

Single-Day Story	Authors/Directors
Ulysses (1922)	Virginia Woolf
Die Hard (1988)	John Hughes
Mrs. Dalloway (1925)	James Joyce
Rebel Without a Cause (1955)	Philip K. Dick
High Noon (1952)	Nicholas Ray
Ferris Bueller's Day Off (1986)	Fred Zinnemann
Saturday (2005)	John McTiernan
Do Androids Dream of Electric Sheep? (1968)*	Don DeLillo
Cosmopolis (2003)	Haruki Murakami
Seize the Day (1956)	Ian McEwan
After Dark (2004)	Saul Bellow

* This book became the inspiration for the 1982 film *Blade Runner*.

(3) **Unparticular:** Binyavanga Wainaina, a Kenyan author whom *Time Magazine* once named to its annual list of the 100 Most Influential People in the World, wrote an essay for the British magazine *Granta* in 2005 called "How to Write About Africa." It has since become perhaps the most read and shared piece in the publication's more than 120-year history. Written in the same satirical vein as Jonathan Swift's "A Modest Proposal" or headlines from the *Onion*, Wainaina's piece exposes the ugly and inaccurate stereotypes many rely on when writing about Africa. Here's a sample of his "advice":

> Never have a picture of a well-adjusted African on the cover of your book, or in it, unless that African has won the Nobel Prize. An AK-47, prominent ribs, naked breasts: use these. If you must include an African, make sure you get one in Masai or Zulu or Dogon dress.

It gets better:

> In your text, treat Africa as if it were one country. It is hot and dusty with rolling grasslands and huge herds of animals and tall, thin people who are starving. Or it is hot and steamy with very short people who eat primates. Don't get bogged down with precise descriptions.

That last line—"Don't get bogged down with precise descriptions"—is such a great way to highlight just how important precise descriptions are, especially when writing or talking about a topic as vulnerable to pernicious generalizations as Africa. The next lines reinforce this point. They also provide a really helpful bit of vocabulary: "unparticular."

> Africa is big: fifty-four countries, [more than a billion] people who are too busy starving and dying and warring and emigrating to read your book. The continent is full

of deserts, jungles, highlands, savannahs, and many other things, but your reader doesn't care about all that, so keep your descriptions romantic and evocative and <u>unparticular</u>.

What are some other topics that tend to be written about in ways that are "unparticular"?

What is one thing you have read or watched recently that, in a bad way, didn't use precise descriptions?

(4) **State of the Union:** It has become a kind of tradition for an "ordinary" citizen—and sometimes more than one—to attend the State of the Union Address as the president's guest. Then at some point during the speech, the television cameras focus on the person as the president talks about some remarkable deed she performed or some specific way a proposed bill will affect the person's life. It can be a moving demonstration of the power of the particular, one person's story standing in for the (mostly) unacknowledged experience of a whole country.

Which president started this tradition? As a hint, here is a transcript from the first time it was done:

> Just two weeks ago, in the midst of a terrible tragedy on the Potomac, we saw again the spirit of American heroism at its finest—the heroism of dedicated rescue workers saving crash victims from icy waters. And we saw the heroism of one of our young government employees, Lenny Skutnik, who, when he saw a woman lose her grip on the helicopter line, dived into the water and dragged her to safety.

(5) **Caddy Compson:** William Faulkner frequently told people that the idea for one of his most famous novels came from a specific mental image: a little girl with dirty underwear who had climbed a tree to look into the second-story window of a house. Faulkner maintained he wrote the novel to find out who the girl was and how she ended up in the tree. He ended up naming her "Caddy Compson."

What's the novel?
- (A) *Absalom, Absalom!*
- (B) *The Light in August*
- (C) *As I Lay Dying*
- (D) *The Sound and the Fury*
- (E) *The Sanctuary*

EXAMPLES SECTION

For Jon [Stewart] the jokes had to be in conversational language, but powerful conversational language. That's where I really learned how to write. He used to say things like, "Specificity is key." In other words, if you're making a joke about, "Why don't you have another ice cream cone?" if you say, "Why don't you have another tub of rum raisin?" it gets funnier because now you're specific in the flavor. He'd go, "What do I preach?" I'd go, "Specificity."

—Rory Albanese, quoted by Chris Smith in *The Daily Show (the Book): An Oral History as Told by Jon Stewart, the Correspondents, Staff and Guests* (2016)

The Power of the Particular: Examples

(1) **Justice Holmes:** "We must think things not words, or at least we must constantly translate our words into the facts for which they stand, if we are to keep to the real and the true."

—Oliver Wendell Holmes Jr., "Law in Science and Science in Law" (1899)

(2) **Readable Writing:** "Whenever you write about a general principle, show its application in a specific case; quote the way someone stated it; tell a pointed anecdote."

—Rudolf Flesch, *The Art of Readable Writing* (1949)

(3) **Popcorn:** "What is real / is the popcorn / jammed between our teeth."

—Linda Pastan, "Popcorn" (1975)

(4) **Anton Chekhov:** "In descriptions of Nature one must seize on small details, grouping them so that when the reader closes his eyes, he gets a picture. For instance, you'll have a moonlit night

if you write that on the mill-dam a piece of glass from a broken bottle glittered like a bright star, and that the black shadow of a dog or a wolf rolled past like a ball."

—Anton Chekhov, letter to his brother Alexander (1886)

(5) **Upper Left-Hand Brick:** "One of them, a girl with strong-lensed glasses, wanted to write a five-hundred-word essay about the United States. He was used to the sinking feeling that comes from statements like this, and suggested without disparagement that she narrow it down to just Bozeman[, Montana].

"When the paper came due she didn't have it and was quite upset. She had tried and tried but she just couldn't think of anything to say.

"He had already discussed her with her previous instructors and they'd confirmed his impressions of her. She was very serious, disciplined and hardworking, but extremely dull. Not a spark of creativity in her anywhere. Her eyes, behind the thick-lensed glasses, were the eyes of a drudge. She wasn't bluffing him, she really couldn't think of anything to say, and was upset by her inability to do as she was told.

"It just stumped him. Now he couldn't think of anything to say. A silence occurred, and then a peculiar answer: 'Narrow it down to the main street of Bozeman.' It was a stroke of insight.

"She nodded dutifully and went out. But just before her next class she came back in real distress, tears this time, distress that had obviously been there for a long time. She still couldn't think of anything to say, and couldn't understand why, if she couldn't think of anything about all of Bozeman, she should be able to think of something about just one street.

"He was furious. 'You're not looking!' he said. A memory came back of his own dismissal from the University for having too much to say. For every fact there is an infinity of hypotheses. The more you look the more you see. She really wasn't looking and yet somehow didn't understand this. He told her angrily, 'Narrow it down to the front of one building on the main street of Bozeman. The Opera House. Start with the upper left-hand brick.'

"Her eyes, behind the thick-lensed glasses, opened wide. She came in the next class with a puzzled look and handed him a five-thousand-word essay on the front of the Opera House on the main street of Bozeman, Montana. 'I sat in the hamburger stand across the street,' she said, 'and started writing about the first brick, and the second brick, and then by the third brick it all started to come and I couldn't stop. They thought I was crazy, and they kept kidding me, but here it all is.'"

—Robert Pirsig, *Zen and the Art of Motorcycle Maintenance* (1974)

(6) **Maggots in Bedsores:** "Fassin relates the words of a young woman volunteer in Alexandra township; asked what was most distressing about her work with AIDS patients, she replied with a directness he found devastating: 'The hardest in this work is when you find maggots in the bedsores.'"

—Hilary Mantel, "Saartjie Baartman's Ghost" (2007)

(7) **Legal Argument:** "One significant detail, made <u>seen</u>, beats forty epithets."

—Karl Llewellyn, *Materials of Legal Argument* (1957)

(8) **Nelson Algren:** "Asked why he stuck to the west side of Chicago for his work, [Nelson Algren] once said, 'A writer does well if in his lifetime he can tell the story of one street.'"

—Art Shay, *Chicago's Nelson Algren* (2007)

PRACTICE SECTION

The sincerity and marrow of the man [Michel de Montaigne] reaches to his
sentences. . . . Cut these words, and they would bleed; they are vascular and alive.
—Ralph Waldo Emerson, "Montaigne; or, the Skeptic" (1850)

Practice Section #1: Strive for Five

Background

The sense of sight is not the only sense good writing evokes. There are four others that can be just as powerful: sound, smell, touch, and taste. Sadly, however, these senses are often neglected. We frequently just stick to what we can see, forgetting that there are many other ways of experiencing the world. This assignment is designed to help you overcome that sensory amnesia.

Assignment: Part I

Find a story you wrote in the past three years. The story can be the fact section of a brief or memo. The story can be the personal statement you used to get into law school or to apply for a fellowship. The story can be pretty much anything you want. It can be personal, political, scary, uplifting—whatever. It doesn't have to be long. It doesn't have to be polished. It just has to contain some bits of narrative description.

Once you find your story, read it over with five different-colored pens or highlighters nearby, one for each sense. Use them to indicate the answers to these questions:

- Where have I triggered the reader's sense of sight?
- Where have I triggered the reader's sense of sound?
- Where have I triggered the reader's sense of smell?
- Where have I triggered the reader's sense of touch?
- Where have I triggered the reader's sense of taste?

A good story will be covered in many colors by the end of this exercise. A terrible story will likely be covered in only one. Try not to be someone who tells terrible stories.

Assignment: Part II

Once you have labeled all the triggered senses in your story, take stock of which ones are underrepresented. Some may be missing entirely. Address this deficiency by revising your story.

This may mean adding a few words, a few sentences, even a few paragraphs. As a result, the structure of your story may shift out of shape. That's okay. You don't have to hand the new version of your story in to anyone. You don't have to worry, at least for this exercise, about making everything cohere. You are simply taking some time to practice how to capture and create a more compelling range of details. Seeing is believing—but seeing, smelling, hearing, tasting, *and* touching is far more effective.

As a final bit of inspiration, here is another helpful reminder from Mary Karr's *The Art of Memoir*: "In writing a scene, you must help the reader employ smell and taste and touch as well as image and noise."

Practice Section #2: "My Favorite Things"
Background

In the movie version of *The Sound of Music*, the character played by Julie Andrews sings a now-iconic song called "My Favorite Things." The items she lists are very particular. Here are a few:

- "raindrops on roses"
- "whiskers on kittens"
- "girls in white dresses with blue satin sashes"

Assignment

Make your own list of favorite things—or rather, make multiple lists, each one a kind of subcategory of what could be a more general list. Here are some possibilities based on what students have done in the past:

- My Favorite Things About Sleeping In
- My Favorite Things About [Insert Favorite Restaurant]
- My Favorite Things About [Insert Favorite Movie, Book, or Television Show]
- My Favorite Things About My Daughter's Laugh

You can steal these lists. You can also modify them to better fit your own interests and experiences. Or you can certainly ignore them altogether. Just be sure that when you make your own lists, you use them as a chance to practice being particular.

Practice Section #3: The Pleasures of Hating

Background

The Belgian-American writer Laure-Anne Bosselaar has a charming poem called "The Pleasures of Hating." It appears in her 2001 book *The Sounds of Grief.* Here is a sample of things she hates:

- "men in black knee socks"
- "stickers on tomatoes"
- "roadblocks"
- "bra-clasps that draw dents in your back"

Assignment

Make a list that reflects your own "Pleasures of Hating." Try to match Bosselaar's precision and range.

SIX

Uselessly Accurate

*There is an accuracy that defeats
itself by the overemphasis of details. . . .
The sentence may be so overloaded
with all its possible qualifications that
it will tumble down of its own weight.*

—Justice Benjamin Cardozo,
*Law and Literature and Other
Essays and Addresses* (1925)

Uselessly Accurate: Concept

What makes writing so difficult? Isn't it the blind craze to say too much?
—Anzia Yezierska, *Bread Givers* (1925)

From the first word of the first sentence in an actual composition, the writer is choosing, selecting, and deciding (most importantly) what to leave out.
—John McPhee, "Writing by Omission" (2015)

People have a tendency to be uselessly accurate, especially when they write. Lawyers are especially guilty. Many pack their memos and briefs with a lot of information that, although perfectly true and well supported, does nothing to advance their argument or sharpen their analysis. Most of the time, this information just ends up being distracting.

The problem is different than the problem of including inappropriate details—or "TMI." TMI involves failures of discretion and decorum. Useless accuracy, on the other hand, involves failures of scope and specificity. The story of how 7 Up got its name provides a good example.

When Charles Leiper Grigg invented 7 Up back in 1929, he initially called it "Bib-Label Lithiated Lemon-Lime Soda." That's uselessly accurate. Yes, the drink had a lemon-lime flavor. Yes, it was a soda. And yes, it was lithiated, meaning it contained lithium citrate. But no, we don't need all that information in the title.

Grigg's next attempt wasn't much better: "7 Up Lithiated Lemon Soda." It wasn't until 1936 that he decided to go simply with "7 Up," a name that has delighted—and intrigued—consumers ever since. There's a lot of speculation, for instance, about whether the "7" in 7 Up comes from

(1) the seven ingredients that originally made up the drink,

(2) the seven-ounce bottles originally used to sell the drink, or

(3) Grigg's (largely facetious) boast that it would cure life's "seven hangovers."

Nobody knows for sure. All we do know is that as a name, "7 Up" is much, *much* better than "Bib-Label Lithiated Lemon-Lime Soda." The other information is uselessly accurate.

Being a Bore

Useless accuracy isn't the worst problem to have, particularly in an era of "fake news" and "alternative facts." At least uselessly accurate information is still accurate. Yet this penchant for hyperinclusion, for stuffing writing with unnecessary facts and data, can have significant negative consequences for the intended audience.

Like boredom, for example.

Nothing loses your reader faster—whether she be a judge, a teacher, or a colleague—than an overabundance of details. "The secret to being a bore," Voltaire wrote back in 1737, "is to tell everything."

But being uselessly accurate creates another problem as well, one that can be even more costly in both the academic and the professional world. It leaves less room to be helpfully persuasive, which is often the main goal when it comes not just to writing a legal brief but also to writing an application essay, or writing a grant proposal, or writing all kinds of other documents, including research papers, résumés, and cover letters. When limited by a word or page limit—as students and professionals often are—writing becomes a zero-sum game. Every time you include one word or phrase, you can't include another word or phrase.

Which is why writers of all kinds might benefit from the "Need-to-Know Principle": What does a judge (or fellowship committee, or employer, or investor) need to know to decide in your favor? Everything else, delete.

The principle works particularly well with law students and young attorneys. Not in the sense of giving them a precise formula for fig-uring out what various decision-makers need to know and what they don't. That kind of knowledge primarily comes with experience, with trial and error, with informed guidance from good teachers and mentors, with time. Rather, the Need-to-Know principle works well in that it helps writers remember that their readers are likely busy people with a lot on their minds and little patience for irrelevant material. "Sentences are attention economies," the rhetorician Rich-ard Lanham has noted. Writing something that is uselessly accurate is therefore not just an affront to style; it is an affront to efficiency. It's giving your readers empty calories. It's making them use a product with unnecessary parts.

Take this description of a lawsuit's procedural history. It's from an appellate brief written by two Michigan Law students who worked in the same unemployment insurance clinic mentioned in chapter 1:

> On October 15, 2015, the Agency issued a Redetermination stating that Ms. Southey was disqualified from receiving ben-efits under § 29.1(a) of the statute. On October 20, 2015, Ms. Southey timely appealed the Redetermination. An Admin-istrative Law Judge conducted a telephone hearing on the mat-ter on December 16, 2015, and issued an Order affirming the Agency's October 15, 2015, Redetermination on December 18, 2015. On January 17, 2016, Ms. Southey requested a rehear-ing on the matter. On January 21, 2016, the Administrative Law Judge issued an Order denying Ms. Southey's request for rehearing.

We are only one paragraph into a section that ultimately stretches to three paragraphs, and yet we are already overwhelmed with unnec-essary parts. Does the judge need to know the specific date of every filing, every hearing, every action that was pursued? All these dates are, of course, accurate. But few are useful. They don't need to be there. They don't do any explanatory or persuasive work. They just take up space.

A rewrite gets closer to what a judge might want:

> On October 15, 2015, the Agency issued a Redetermination stating that Ms. Southey was disqualified from receiving benefits. Ms. Southey timely appealed. An Administrative Law Judge conducted a telephone hearing and eventually issued an Order affirming the Agency's Redetermination. Ms. Southey's request for a rehearing was denied.

Note the size difference between the paragraphs. The original version was 92 words. The rewrite is 47. That's a big gain in efficiency. Imagine if you could do that with all your paragraphs—or at least some of them. Imagine how much time and mental energy you would save your readers.

Maximally Considerate

Being uselessly accurate is fortunately the type of problem where awareness can be an antidote. Simply introducing "uselessly accurate" as a common infirmity makes many of my students smile in recognition. It's as if they had been struggling with an unknown condition for many years and now finally have a name for what's been afflicting them. They also soon start to write more purposeful sentences.

Even more effective is adding the term "helpfully persuasive" to create the following spectrum:

Uselessly Accurate ⟵—————⟶ Helpfully Persuasive

There is something about the visual distance between these two terms that helps writers realize (1) accuracy is a necessary but not sufficient element when it comes to persuasion, (2) there needs to be a compelling reason for every fact and figure their drafts include, and (3) in the end, writing is about selection and a kind of strategic restraint that is also, at its core, deeply courteous. David Foster Wallace once made this point quite well in a piece that came out of his own experience teaching students to write better: "'Formal writing' does not mean gratuitously fancy writing; it means clean, clear, maximally considerate writing."

It would be nice to think Charles Leiper Grigg was being maximally considerate when he deleted "Bib-Label Lithiated Lemon-Lime Soda" from the name of his soft drink. It would be nice to think he eventually said to his marketing team, "Look, all the consumer needs to know is that the drink is called '7 Up.' Everything else, delete."

QUESTIONS SECTION

How long is a good idea?

　　—Verlyn Klinkenborg, *Several Short Sentences About Writing* (2012)

Uselessly Accurate: Questions*

(1) **Design:** In 1977, a small computer company advertised the launch of its new personal computer in a marketing brochure. On the cover of the brochure were these words: "Simplicity is the ultimate sophistication." Name the company.

　　(A) IBM

　　(B) Atari

　　(C) Microsoft

　　(D) Apple

(2) **Conspicuous Composition:** H. L. Mencken, the author of *The American Language* and a longtime journalist for the *Baltimore Sun*, once described the overstuffed writing of a famous economist this way: "To say what might have been said on a postage stamp, _____ took more than a page in a book." Identify the economist.

　　(A) John Meynard Keynes

　　(B) Milton Friedman

　　(C) Adam Smith

　　(D) Thorstein Veblen

　　[Hint: The economist is famous for the concept of "conspicuous consumption."]

---

* For answers, see page 226 of Appendix C.

(3) **Time Saver:** Stephen Walt is a professor of international relations at Harvard's Kennedy School of Government. Writing for *Foreign Policy* in 2013, Walt took on the topic of, in his words, "why academic writing is frequently abysmal." Toward the end of his essay, he offers this directive: "Academics should strive to write clearly for the obvious reason that it will allow many others to learn more quickly. Think of it this way: If I spend 20 extra hours editing, re-writing, and polishing a piece of research, and if that extra effort enables 500 people to spend a half-hour less apiece figuring out what I am saying, then I have saved humankind a net 230 hours of effort."

Walt's hypothetical can be applied to other kinds of writing as well. Think of that last thing you wrote that was read by multiple people. Maybe it was a memo. Maybe it was a grant proposal. Maybe it was a résumé or email or blog post. What if 30 minutes of extra editing on your part could have saved each of those readers 5, 10, even 20 minutes each? How many net hours could you have saved humankind?

Or think about it another way: What was the last thing you read written by someone you wish would have spent more time editing what they wrote? What could you have done with the time they could have saved you? To make this question more concrete:

- How many loads of laundry could you have done?
- How many friends could you have called back?
- How many emails could you have written?
- How much of a movie, or television show, or podcast, or book could you have enjoyed?
- How many meals could you have prepared?
- How much longer could you have slept in this morning?

(4) **Syllable Saver:** Several 20th-century American poets are known for their compressed, economical style. Praising the work of one of these poets, the literary critic Albert Mobilio observed that in his poems "scarcely a syllable is wasted." Identify the poet.

(A) Walt Whitman
(B) Pablo Neruda
(C) Ernest Hemingway
(D) Robert Frost
(E) Robert Creeley

(5) **Clutter:** In *On Writing Well*, longtime journalist and writing teacher William Zinsser identifies "clutter" as "the disease of American writing":

> We are a society strangling in unnecessary words, circular constructions, pompous frills and meaningless jargon. Who can understand the viscous language of everyday American commerce and enterprise: the business letter, the interoffice memo, the corporation report, the notice from the bank explaining its latest "simplified" statement?

He then shares what he calls the secret of good writing: "strip every sentence to its cleanest components." To explain what he means, he offers the observations below. See if you can fill out the paragraph below using the Word Bank.

Every word that serves no _____, every long word that could be a short word, every adverb that carries the same meaning that is already in the verb, every passive construction that leaves the reader _____ of who is doing what: these are the thousand and one adulterants that _____ the strength of a sentence. And they usually occur, ironically, in proportion to _____ and rank.

Word Bank: weaken, unsure, education, function

Now read a passage from a different one of Zinsser's books, *Writing to Learn*. Try to identify (and eliminate) at least 5 of the 11 unnecessary words I've added to it. In other words, try to "declutter" it in the way that Zinsser might.

Far too many Americans are prevented from doing useful work because they never really learned to fully express themselves. Contrary to what is the general belief, writing isn't something that only "writers" do; writing is a basic skill for getting through life. Yet most American adults are absolutely terrified of the prospect—ask a middle-aged engineer to write up a report and you'll see something close to panic. Writing, however, isn't a special language that belongs only to English teachers and a few other sensitive and educated souls who have a "gift for words." Writing is thinking on paper. Anyone who thinks clearly should be able to write clearly—about any subject in the world at all.

EXAMPLES SECTION

Try to leave out the parts that readers tend to skip.
—Elmore Leonard, *Elmore Leonard's 10 Rules of Writing* (2007)

Uselessly Accurate: Examples

(1) **Kurt Vonnegut:** "Your eloquence should be the servant of the ideas in your head. Your rule might be this: If a sentence, no matter how excellent, does not illuminate your subject in some new and useful way, scratch it out."
—Kurt Vonnegut, "How to Write with Style" (1985)

(2) **Classical Music:** "It is not hard to compose. But it is wonderfully hard to let superfluous notes fall under the table."
—Johannes Brahms, quoted by Julius H. Jacobson
in *The Classical Musical Experience* (2005)

(3) **Design:** "I start with a thousand different thoughts. One by one I throw them all out until at the end I am left with one or two or three that are essential to the whole question. The abstraction for me is this idea of getting rid of everything that is not essential to making a point."
—Christoph Niemann, "Abstract: The Art of Design" (2016)

(4) **Mark Twain:** "Anybody can have ideas—the difficulty is to express them without squandering a quire of paper on an idea that ought to be reduced to one glittering paragraph."
—Mark Twain, letter to Emeline Beach (1868)

(5) **Susan Sontag:** "My first draft usually has only a few elements worth keeping. I have to find what those are and build from them and throw out what doesn't work, or what simply is not alive."

—Susan Sontag, quoted by Charles Ruas in
Conversations with American Writers (1985)

(6) **Judicial Opinions:** "Frankly, in writing an opinion, it's important to be economical. People will not read long opinions. The genius of Oliver Wendell Holmes lay in his ability to convey meaning succinctly."

—Justice Stephen Breyer, quoted by Ben
Yagoda in *The Sound on the Page* (2005)

(7) **Physics:** "There is beauty in simplicity. And it is even more beautiful when that beauty condenses out of simplicity."

—Helen Czerski, *Storm in a Teacup: The
Physics of Everyday Life* (2016)

(8) **Thinking Like a Writer:** "[To progress as a legal writer], you must pass through the law's convolutions and emerge on the other side, capable of a clarity that rests on a new and sophisticated form of simplicity. This simplicity has nothing to do with over-simplification. In part, it results from developing the legal judgment and courage to focus on the essential core of an issue."

—Stephen Armstrong and Timothy Terrell, *Thinking Like a
Writer: A Lawyer's Guide to Effective Writing and Editing* (2008)

PRACTICE SECTION

I went from being a bad writer to a good writer after taking a one-day course in "business writing." I couldn't believe how simple it was. I'll tell you the main tricks here so you don't have to waste a day in class.

Business writing is about clarity and persuasion. The main technique is keeping things simple. Simple writing is persuasive. A good argument in five sentences will sway more people than a brilliant argument in a hundred sentences. Don't fight it.

Simple means getting rid of extra words.

—Scott Adams (creator of *Dilbert*),
"The Day You Became a Better Writer" (2007)

Practice Section #1: 100 Words

Background
Take a look at some things you have written recently. Then search them for 100 unnecessary words. The 100 words can't be from the same document. They can't even be from just two documents. They have to be collected by editing at least three different documents.

Emails count. So do tweets and other social media posts. The reach of useless accuracy extends beyond formal modes of writing.

Assignment
To register your total, create a document that has

- the original sentence or phrase
- the new sentence or phrase
- the unnecessary words you deleted

Practice Section #2: Meat and Potatoes

Background

Supreme Court Justice Clarence Thomas was once asked why his opinions were 25% shorter, on average, than the opinions of the other justices on the bench. Here was his response: "Editing, editing, editing. [My law clerks and I] do a lot of editing, and it's very aggressive. We eliminate a lot of trivial nonsense. And I do not like cuteness in my opinions. You save that for your own stuff. It is all meat and potatoes."

Assignment

Give me meat and potatoes. Take something you've written and make it at least 25% shorter than the original. So if the original was a 10-page memo, make the edited version a 7.5-page memo. And if the original was a 4-paragraph email, make the edited version a 3-paragraph email. Focus on the bare essentials. No garnish. No fluff.

Every word needs an unobjectionable reason for being spared your "Delete" button. If there is any doubt that a word is not doing meaningful work in a sentence, phrase, or heading, it gets cut.

* * *

For inspiration, take a look at a literary gem James Joyce once called "one of the best stories ever written": Ernest Hemingway's "A Clean, Well-Lighted Place." Or read something by Lydia Davis, who is even more extreme than Hemingway when it comes to purposeful compression.

You might also, to get in the right mind-set, consider this exercise the writing equivalent of

- lightening the contents of your backpack by 25% before a big hike
- freeing your closet of 25% of its clothes during a spring cleaning
- reducing your spending by 25%
- clearing out 25% of your garage

There are going to be some hard choices. You may find it difficult to part with everything you need to. But the process will be a good counterpoint to the "Power of the Particular" chapter, where you might have felt encouraged to experiment with excess. It will also teach you to be resourceful. Some 4-word expressions can become 3-word expressions if you just think more deliberately and creatively about what each of those words could be. Train your editorial brain to send you this message as you reexamine every word, sentence, and paragraph in your document: "You know, you might not actually need that."

SEVEN

Corresponding Ideas in Corresponding Forms

You campaign in poetry.
You govern in prose.

—Mario Cuomo, quoted in an
interview in the *New Republic* (1985)

Corresponding Ideas in Corresponding Forms: Concept

A moment's insight is sometimes worth a life's experience.
  —Oliver Wendell Holmes Sr., *The Professor at the Breakfast Table* (1859)

Great Faces. Great Places.
  —license plate slogan in South Dakota

Don't make the mistake of thinking that content always comes before structure. You don't need to figure out all of your ideas before you figure out how you are going to organize them. A lot of value can come from going in the opposite direction: first figure out how you are going to organize your ideas—first figure out the appropriate structure—and then figure out the appropriate content.

I often make this point to law students by offering them the following suggestion: "Once you find the right structure, perhaps it will be easier to find the right content."

My hope is that even if they continue to start with content, even if they continue to insist that information always trumps organization, they'll at least start to appreciate the strong relationship between the architecture of that information and the information itself. It's like the relationship between (1) the blueprints for a building and (2) the people and furniture that will eventually go inside. Each affects the other. The influence is not one-way.

Patrick Henry and Malcolm X

When it comes to advocacy, one of the most useful structures is parallel structure. Think of the famous appeal by the Virginian Patrick Henry during the American Revolution. On March 23, 1775, Henry addressed some of the most powerful leaders in the colonies. They were all meeting as delegates of the Second Virginia Convention at St. John's Church in Richmond. George Washington was there. So was Thomas Jefferson.

Henry's goal was clear: he wanted Virginia to take military action against the British. "We must fight!" he said at one point. "I repeat it sir, we must fight! An appeal to arms and to the God of hosts is all that is left to us." What he added at the end, with a voice as booming as it was passionate, has helped make this speech one of the most celebrated in American history: "Give me liberty or give me death!"

Note how perfectly that statement uses parallel structure. On one side of the phrase, you get a verb ("give"), and on the other side of the phrase, you get a verb ("give").

Give   me   liberty   or   give   me   death

(verb)   *(verb)*

On one side of the phrase, you get a pronoun ("me"), and on the other side of the phrase, you get a pronoun ("me").

Give   me   liberty   or   give   me   death

(verb) **(pronoun)**   *(verb)* **(pronoun)**

Finally, on one side of the phrase, you get a regular noun ("liberty"), and on the other side of the phrase, you get a regular noun ("death").

Give   me   liberty   or   give   me   death

(verb) **(pronoun)** (noun)   *(verb)* **(pronoun)** (noun)

The symmetry is exact, like entering a football stadium at the fifty-yard line or seeing a seesaw evenly balanced by two eight-year-olds, each precisely the same weight as the other.

A more technical way to describe this kind of arrangement comes from Karl Claus, who taught for many years at the famed Iowa Writers' Workshop. In *A Self Made of Words: Creating a Distinctive Persona in Nonfiction Writing*, Klaus includes a whole chapter on parallel structure. He defines it this way: "corresponding ideas expressed in corresponding forms."

Advertising slogans can be a good place to see this correspondence at work:

Home Depot: "More saving. More doing."

Botox: "Keep the wisdom. Lose the lines."

Virgin America: "Fly like a CEO. Pay like a temp."

Take the period in each slogan as the dividing line. What you get on one side ("More saving") mirrors, at least structurally, what you get on the other ("More doing").

You can also see this correspondence in the title of a speech given by Malcolm X on April 3, 1964, at the Cory Methodist Church in Cleveland, Ohio. The country, divided over the issues of civil rights, was preparing for a big election later that year. So Malcolm encouraged the largely African American crowd to think strategically about how to use their vote, especially given that the country's demographics meant that African Americans could play a major role. The way he communicates this point closes with a cleverly evocative bit of parallel structure.

What does this mean? It means that when white people are evenly divided, and black people have a block of votes of their own, it is left up to them to determine who's going to sit <u>in the White House</u> and who's going to be <u>in the dog house</u>.

As well structured as this passage is, the title of the speech is the real gem: "The Ballot or the Bullet." Not only do the syllables line up— three syllables to the left side of "or" and three to the right—but Malcolm also adds in some connective alliteration. The "B" that begins "Ballot" and the "B" that begins "Bullet" help reinforce the parallelism.

He could have called the speech "The Ballot or the Gun" or "The Ballot or the Ammunition." Just like he could have called it "The Vote or the Bullet" or "The Election or the Bullet." But none of those would have been as effective as "The Ballot or the Bullet." None would have made use of the kind of symmetry that is an aid to comprehension; the kind that makes it easy to process information quickly, even instantaneously; the kind that the 17th-century philosopher and mathematician Blaise Pascal might have been talking about when he observed that "symmetry is what we see at a glance."

At a Glance

The idea that symmetry is an aid to comprehension—that it can help your audience grasp an idea or argument "at a glance," with little mental effort—is good to remember when trying to clean up clunky sentences. We'll soon look at an example from a green card application written by a law student in the University of Michigan Human Trafficking Clinic.

The clinic represents trafficking victims from around the world in a wide range of legal matters. Sometimes this means preparing them to testify against their traffickers in criminal trials. Sometimes it means initiating lawsuits through which victims can sue their traffickers themselves. And oftentimes, as we'll see in the green card example, it means guiding victims through the not-always-easy-to-navigate world of immigration law.

The client in the example, a 36-year-old woman from Haiti we'll call "Elise," had already moved pretty far along in that world. She had been granted a special kind of visa reserved for trafficking victims under the Trafficking Victims Protection Act, as well as the accompanying right to pursue a green card—a document that is a kind of immigration golden ticket: it would allow her to permanently live and work in the US.

The green card application includes a section for background facts. Trying to explain that Elise had spent 18 years working in South

America as a domestic servant before being trafficked in the United States by a family that (falsely) promised to help her become a citizen, the student wrote these sentences:

> Before coming to the United States, Elise worked as a domestic servant for eighteen years. She worked in French Guiana for six of those years and the other twelve in Brazil.

These sentences aren't terrible. All the information is correct. All the necessary data are included. But you may have noticed a kind of grammatical glitch as you moved from the first part of the second sentence ("She worked in French Guiana for six of those years") to the second part ("and the other twelve in Brazil").

The glitch isn't major. You can still understand what is being communicated. But we can make things easier on the readers, who in this case hold Elise's fate very much in their hands, by smoothing out the transition. We don't want the immigration officials to experience any kind of stumble. Instead, we want the sentences to be as user-friendly as possible. Parallel structure can help.

The key is to get the order of the words to align. Start by focusing on the preposition "in." It appears both in the first part of the sentence ("She worked in French Guiana for six of those years") and in the second part of the sentence ("and the other twelve in Brazil."). Each time, it is placed next to the name of a country, which is helpful when it comes to parallel structure.

The problem is that in the first part of the sentence, "in French Guiana" comes before the reader learns the amount of years Elise spent working there ("in French Guiana for six of those years")—while in the second part, "in Brazil" comes after the reader learns that information ("the other twelve in Brazil"). Notice what happens when we align the parts of the sentence more directly. Notice what happens when we use parallel structure:

Before coming to the United States, Elise worked as a domestic servant for eighteen years. She worked <u>in French Guiana for six of those years</u> and <u>in Brazil for the other twelve</u>.

Isn't that a little easier on your eyes and brain? Doesn't it allow you to grasp the information more quickly—maybe even "at a glance"?

A Tale of Two Sentences

In 1984, researchers at Yale and the University of Massachusetts tested the effect of parallel structure on reading time and comprehension. They found that "readers and listeners strongly prefer coordinated elements of sentences to be parallel in structure."

The pervasiveness of this "parallel structure effect" is what struck the researchers the most. They tried out several different sentence constructions. Some constructions used active voice; some used passive voice. Some used animate nouns; some used inanimate nouns. In each, the parallel version was more easily absorbed than the nonparallel version. "These observations suggest," the researchers concluded, "that the preference for parallel structure . . . is not simply an aesthetic judgment about the elegance of various sentence forms." Structure actually helps people understand what you are trying to communicate.

Perhaps this is why Abraham Lincoln used parallel structure when writing to the future vice-president of the Confederate States, Alex Stephens, two days after South Carolina became the first state to secede from the Union:

<u>You think slavery is right and ought to be extended</u>, while <u>we think it is wrong and ought to be restricted</u>. That, I suppose, is the rub. It certainly is the only substantial difference between us.

Perhaps it is also why Frederick Douglass used parallel structure throughout his written accounts of his life as a slave, as well as in many of his speeches—including one in Williamsport, Pennsylvania on November 15, 1867, that seems like a rhetorical relative of Malcolm X's own "The Ballot or the Bullet" speech mentioned above. "A man's rights rest in three boxes," Douglass said. "The ballot box, jury box, and cartridge box. <u>Let no man be kept from the ballot box because of his color.</u> <u>Let no woman be kept from the ballot box because of her sex.</u>"

There is a clarity that comes with parallel structure when it is used in this way. There is a built-in sense of order and authority.

The literary theorist and former *New York Times* columnist Stanley Fish highlights these qualities when discussing parallel structure in his 2011 book *How to Write a Sentence*. Parallel structure, he suggests, is one of the key ingredients when you want to express "unshakeable conviction." Keep your sentences short, he advises, employ parallel structure, use the present tense, limit yourself to relatively small words.

Sentences with those characteristics "are rhythmic in feel and easy to remember; they can be delivered in a click and a snap." They are perfect for crafting a "pithy pronouncement of wisdom in a manner that does not invite disagreement."

Supreme Court justices have learned this lesson well. In 1970, as tensions over the war in Vietnam mounted, the justices had to decide whether to overturn the conviction of 19-year-old Robert Cohen, who had been arrested for wearing an intentionally provocative antiwar jacket into a Los Angeles courthouse. On the back of the jacket, stenciled in red ink, read the words "Fuck the draft."

Deciding in favor of Cohen and making clear that the First Amendment protects speech that some may find offensive, Justice John Marshall Harlan used a form of parallel structure to craft exactly the kind of pithy pronouncement Fish describes. "One man's vulgarity," Harlan wrote, "is another's lyric."

Justice Oliver Wendell Holmes took a similar approach in *New York Trust v. Eisner*, a decision in which the Court upheld the constitutionality of a federal estate tax. It wasn't a very memorable case, but it did produce an extremely memorable—and wonderfully parallel—maxim: "A page of history is worth a pound of logic."

I obviously don't know whether Harlan or Holmes came up with the structure of these pithy pronouncements before settling on the content out of which they were made. My guess is that the structure and content arrived in quick succession, if not simultaneously—the way a clever line might to a seasoned comedian. Both justices were avid readers. Both likely internalized, early on, the elegant effect of putting corresponding ideas in corresponding forms, even if neither would have necessarily used that phrase to describe what they were doing.

But if you are just starting out as a writer, or are simply looking to improve the effectiveness with which you communicate, it can be helpful to make a more deliberate effort to add parallel structure to your writerly repertoire. So try to keep in mind the core principle: "corresponding ideas in corresponding forms." It's a great way to deliver information.

QUESTIONS SECTION

Why was I so authoritative in a surgeon's coat but so meek in a patient's gown?
—Paul Kalanithi, *When Breath Becomes Air* (2016)

Corresponding Ideas in Corresponding Forms: Questions*

(1) **Politics:** Fill in the missing word or phrase.

"Better to be despised for too anxious apprehensions than _____ by too confident a security."
—Edmund Burke, *Reflections on the French Revolution* (1790)

"When all think alike, _____ thinks very much."
—Walter Lippman, *The Stakes of Diplomacy* (1915)

"I like the dreams of the _____ more than the history of the past. So good night. I will dream on, always fancying that Mrs. Adams and yourself are by my side marking the progress and the obliquities of ages and countries."
—Thomas Jefferson, letter to John Adams (1816)

---

* For answers, see page 227 of Appendix C.

(2) **Poetry:** Unscramble the letters and use them to fill in the blank.

Letters: l a n e o
"Laugh, and the world laughs with you / Weep, and you weep
_____."

—Ella Wheeler Wilcox, "Solitude" (1883)

Letters: c e f n e s
"Good _____ make good neighbors."

—Robert Frost, "Mending Wall" (1914)

Letters: u r p l e y
"I love thee freely, as men strive for right. / I love thee _____,
as they turn from praise."

—Elizabeth Barrett Browning, "How Do I Love Thee?" (1850)

(3) **Marketing:** Match the slogan with the company.

Slogan	Company
"Expect more. Pay less."	Harley Davidson
"Carbs to compete. Electrolytes to replenish."	Target
"American by birth. Rebel by choice."	Gatorade
"Live in your world. Play in ours."	PlayStation
"Your vision. Our future."	Olympus Cameras

(4) **Movies:** Complete the movie tagline.

"She brought a _____ town to its feet and a huge corporation to its _____."

—*Erin Brockovich* (2000)

"Just because they serve you doesn't mean they _____ you."

—*Clerks* (1994)

"The true story of a _____ fake."

—*Catch Me If You Can* (2002)

"The thing that won't die, in the nightmare that won't ____."

—*The Terminator* (1984)

"The world's most dangerous times created the world's most dangerous _____."

—*Straight Outta Compton* (2015)

"Fear can ____ you prisoner. _____ can set you free."

—*Shawshank Redemption* (1994)

"Blood lost. ____ found."

—*The Revenant* (2015)

"At the ____ of the universe lies the beginning of vengeance."

—*Star Trek 2: The Wrath of Khan* (1982)

(5) **Authors:** Identify the author.

"It was the best of times, it was the worst of times."
- (A) Charles Murray
- (B) Charles Baxter
- (C) Charles Dickens
- (D) Ray Charles

"How vain it is to sit down to write when you have not stood up to live."
- (A) Henry Wadsworth Longfellow
- (B) Henry David Thoreau
- (C) Patrick Henry
- (D) Thierry Henry

"The peculiar circumstances of the moment may render a measure more or less wise, but cannot render it more or less constitutional."
- (A) Justice Thurgood Marshall
- (B) Justice John Marshall
- (C) Justice John Marshall Harlan
- (D) Justice John Roberts

EXAMPLES SECTION

The land of the free, and the home of the brave.
—Francis Scott Key, "The Star-Spangled Banner" (1814)

Corresponding Ideas in Corresponding Forms: Examples

(1) **Criminal Justice:** "We have a system that treats you better if you are rich and guilty than if you're poor and innocent."
—Bryan Stevenson, *Just Mercy* (2014)

(2) **Veterans:** "Lose your legs and they give you a medal, lose your mind and they give you nothing."
—Isabel Allende, *Maya's Notebook* (2013)

(3) **Donating Blood:** "The need is constant. The gratification is instant."
—American Red Cross

(4) **First Amendment:** "A criminal statute chills. The prior restraint freezes."
—Alexander Bickel, winning brief in *New York Times vs. United States* (1971) (a.k.a. "The Pentagon Papers Case")

(5) **NFL:** "Playing in the NFL is a blue collar job with white collar pay."
—Michael Rosenberg, "Higher Powers" (2017)

(6) **Warren Buffet:** "The CEO who misleads others in public may eventually mislead himself in private."
—Warren Buffett, letter to shareholders (1983)

(7) **Ludwig Wittgenstein:** "The limits of my language are the limits of my world."

—Ludwig Wittgenstein, *Tractatus Logico-Philosophicus* (1922)

(8) **Attention:** "A wealth of information creates a poverty of attention."

—Herbert Simon, "Designing Organizations for an Information-Rich World" (1971)

PRACTICE SECTION

The more I tell, the more I lose.

—John Updike, *Rabbit, Run* (1960)

Practice Section #1: Agreement

Background

Once you understand parallel structure, you'll be less likely to slip into a mistake I see my students make all the time: using an inconsistent structure when arranging items in a list. Here's an example from a memo detailing the likelihood that a noncompete agreement a baker signed with her former boss would be upheld in court.

> To be upheld, the agreement must not be against public interest, not produce undue hardship on the baker, and must have reasonable restrictions.

You can see the mistake more clearly if you arrange the list in bullet points:

To be upheld, the agreement must

- not be against public interest
- not produce undue hardship on the baker
- must have reasonable restrictions

Each item needs to be able to finish the lead-in words "To be upheld, the agreement must . . . ." The first item does that: "To be upheld, the agreement must not be against public interest." The second item does that: "To be upheld, the agreement must not produce undue hardship on the baker." But we run into a problem with the third item. When read with the lead-in words, that item creates a double "must":

> To be upheld, the agreement <u>must must</u> have reasonable restrictions.

Remembering to put "corresponding ideas in corresponding forms" helps solve that problem. It prompts you to check each item and ask, "Are their structures the same? Do their forms correspond?"

You can create a list, for example, that goes "noun, noun, noun." You can also create a list that goes "adjective, adjective, adjective." But you can't create one that goes "noun, noun, adjective." "Apples, oranges, and bananas" is a perfectly fine list. "Apples, oranges, and salty" is a grammatical mess.

And in a way, that's what the memo about the baker produced: a grammatical mess. The parts of speech are different than in the "apples, oranges, and salty" example. The memo's list was never going to be as straightforward as what "apples, oranges, and salty" should have been, which is "noun, noun, noun." But the principle is the same. Parallel structure was violated. Corresponding ideas were put in confusingly uncorresponding forms. It's as if Patrick Henry had said, "Give me liberty, or give me died."

Here's another example, from a cover letter written by a second-year law student: "This fall, I will be exploring my interest in other areas of the law by taking Evidence, Copyright, and writing for the *Journal of International Law*."

The bullet-pointed list again exposes the culprit:

> This fall, I will be exploring my interest in other areas of the law by taking
>
> • Evidence
> • Copyright
> • writing for the *Journal of International Law*

You can write, "This fall, I will be exploring my interest in other areas of law by taking Evidence." You can write, "This fall, I will be exploring my interest in other areas of the law by taking Copyright." But you can't write, "This fall, I will be exploring my interest in other areas of the law by <u>taking writing</u> for the *Journal of International Law.*" That last item throws the whole arrangement off.

Assignment

Check your writing for inconsistent structures. They often pop up in lists of three or more items. If you spot one, try to smooth out the inconsistency. Typically, this involves changing the last item in the list. But you may have to change other items in the list as well.

To help you practice, try editing the examples below:

Online Bio of Third-Year Law Student

He was a quarterfinalist in the Campbell Moot Court Competition, president of the Sports Law Society, and was managing editor of the *Michigan Journal of International Law.*

Email by Second-Year Law Student

I am excited to learn more about litigation, see what types of advocacy are effective, and to improve my legal writing.

LinkedIn Page of Second-Year Law Student

Lou is also an enormous New York Yankees fan, a lover of history, and never misses an episode of *Saturday Night Live.*

Draft of Book on International Law

The beginning of the 21st century has seen an unprecedented growth in the power and influence of international courts. These courts have increased in number, expanded their scope, and the amount of cases is rapidly multiplying.

Op-ed Printed in the *Washington Post* [It was the text of a law school exam used at the University of Chicago in 2015.]

> That morning, at 9 a.m., Ford Motor Company announces it has secretly moved substantial parts of its operations to Brazil, to take advantage of lower labor costs, laxer regulation, and to avoid retaliation from the soon-to-be president.

Practice Section #2: Omit

Background

An awareness of parallel structure can also help you develop a pair of more advanced writing moves. One involves omitting an implied word or phrase from what would otherwise be a perfect parallel structure construction. The poet Alexander Pope's preface to a translation of the *Iliad* back in 1712 includes two examples of this move in a rather complex sentence that highlights what Pope considers the differences between two towering literary figures: Homer of ancient Greece and Virgil of ancient Rome.

> Homer was the greater genius; Virgil, the better artist; in the one, we most admire the man; in the other, the work.

Without the omission, the sentence would read:

> Homer was the greater genius, Virgil <u>was</u> the better artist; in the one, we most admire the man; in the other, <u>we most admire</u> the work.

The second version isn't bad, and it is certainly nicely symmetric. But Pope's version, with the omission, is at once more succinct and more sophisticated. There is an elegant efficiency to it, a sense that by trimming words you can add style.

Pope achieves the same effect later in the paragraph, after two sentences that exhibit a more traditional parallel structure. Here's the first of those two more traditional sentences:

Homer hurries us with a commanding impetuosity; Virgil leads us with an attractive majesty.

Here's the second:

Homer scatters with a general profusion; Virgil bestows with a careful magnificence.

And here's where Pope opts again for omission:

Homer, like the Nile, pours out his riches with a sudden overflow; Virgil, like a river with its banks, with a constant stream.

Assignment

Find a sentence you've written that would benefit from the omission Pope employs. Or create one in the writing you do this week, whether that be the formal writing you do for work or school, or the informal writing you do communicating with friends and family.

To help your brain recognize the pattern, here are some additional examples from a wide range of sources.

Magazine Article: "The loss of a child is an unbearable grief, the murder of a child an unthinking atrocity."
—Jill Lepore, "Baby Doe" (2016)

Food Memoir: "There is a communion of more than our bodies when bread is broken and wine drunk."
—M. F. K. Fisher, *The Gastronomical Me* (1943)

20th-Century Short Story: "The streets were a furnace, the sun an executioner."
—Cynthia Ozick, "Rosa" (1983)

21st-Century Novel: "The fear was respect; the respect, fear."

—Zadie Smith, *On Beauty* (2005)

Appellate Brief: "Ozzie was nine years old at the time; Zayden only two."

—legal brief in the University of Michigan Child Welfare Appellate Clinic (2016)

Poetry: "Some say the world will end in fire. / Some say in ice."

—Robert Frost, "Fire and Ice" (1920)

Harder Poetry: "This bed thy center is, these walls, thy sphere."

—John Donne, "The Sun Rising" (1633)

Sociology: "Ethnographers shrink themselves in the field but enlarge themselves on the page because first-person accounts convey experience—and experience, authority."

—Matthew Desmond, *Evicted: Poverty and Profit in the American City* (2016)

Forgiveness: "To err is human; to forgive, divine."

—Alexander Pope, "An Essay on Criticism" (1711)

Practice Section #3: Nifty Not

You can't really understand something until you understand what it is not.
—Steven Pinker, *The Stuff of Thought: Language*
as a Window into Human Nature (2007)

Background

The other advanced writing move that parallel structure can help you develop involves the word "not." A good example comes in an ad campaign HBO used a number of years ago to distinguish its programming from the shows you might see on other channels: "It's not TV. It's HBO." Here are some others:

Law: "The life of the law has <u>not</u> been logic; it has been experience."
—Oliver Wendell Holmes Jr., *The Common Law* (1881)

Politics: "The test of our progress is <u>not</u> whether we add more to the abundance of those who have much; it is whether we provide enough for those who have too little."
—Franklin D. Roosevelt, "Second Inaugural Address" (1937)

Business: "This is <u>not</u> a shoe. This is a movement."
—motto of Toms Shoes, which pioneered the idea of "One for One" matching, where a customer's purchase triggers a charitable donation

Sports: "Golf is <u>not</u> just a game you know. Golf is a career advantage."
—David Mitchell, *Cloud Atlas* (2004)

Military: "This was <u>not</u> a war of planning and discipline; it was one of agility and innovation."
> —General Stanley McChrystal (with Tatum Collins, David Silverman, and Chris Fussell), *Team of Teams: New Rules of Engagement for a Complex World* (2015)

Hip-Hop: "I'm <u>not</u> a businessman; I'm a business, man!"
> —Jay-Z, "Diamonds From Sierra Leone" (2005)

Martinis: "Shaken, <u>not</u> stirred."
> —James Bond in *Dr. No* (1962)

Assignment

Find some opportunities to try out this "not." If it helps you remember, you can call it the name my undergraduate students and I used when we first started noticing it as a handy variant of parallel structure: "the nifty not."

But if that name doesn't work for you, use something else. Or use nothing at all. As we will learn later in chapter 10, naming things can aid learning and memory. But that doesn't have to be true for you in every case. My main concern is that you experiment with these moves, develop a certain comfort with them, and then try to make them your own.

EIGHT

Clarity and Coherence

When you write, it's like
braiding your hair. Taking a handful
of coarse unruly strands and attempting
to bring them unity.

—Edwidge Danticat, *Krik? Krak!* (1995)

Clarity and Coherence: Concept

A sentence confuses us when it opens with information that is unexpected.
—Joseph Williams and Gregory Colomb,
Style: Lessons in Clarity and Grace (1991)

In this work are exhibited in a very high degree the two most engaging powers of an author. New things are made familiar and familiar things are made new.
—Samuel Johnson, *Lives of the English Poets* (1781)

If your sentences flow, chances are your ideas will flow. If your ideas flow, people are much more likely to understand you. And if people understand you, they are much more likely to be persuaded by you.

No judge, for example, looks at a poorly written motion submitted by an attorney and says, "This document is so confusing. I think I'll grant it." Just like no teacher looks at a poorly written exam submitted by a student and says, "This thing is really hard to follow. I think I'll give it an A." Obfuscation may sometimes work when trying to publish research in highfalutin academic journals, like when the physicist Alan Sokal tricked the editors of the humanities journal *Social Text* into publishing an article he intentionally filled with fancy-sounding nonsense. But in most circumstances, clarity and coherence reign supreme.

Old → New

Few things improve clarity and coherence more effectively than making sure to transition from old information to new information as you move between and within sentences. An exaggerated example comes from a proverb with origins stretching at least as far back as the 13th century. It's about preparedness and unforeseen consequences. Here's one version:

For want of a nail, the shoe was lost.
For want of a shoe, the horse was lost.
For want of a horse, the knight was lost.

For want of a knight, the battle was lost—
All for want of a nail.

I don't encourage you to write like this. You'll exhaust your reader's patience and probably some of your own. But I do encourage you to embrace the principles built into its linked structure.

Principle 1: "Put at the beginning of a sentence those ideas that you have already mentioned, referred to, or implied, or concepts that you can reasonably assume your reader is familiar with, and will readily recognize." (a.k.a. "Old Information")

Principle 2: "Put at the end of your sentence, the newest, the most surprising, the most significant information that you want to stress—perhaps the information that you will expand on in your next sentence." (a.k.a. "New Information")

Both of these principles come from *Style: Lessons in Clarity and Grace* by Joseph Williams and Gregory Colomb, whose influence on the writing program at the University of Chicago (and many other places) was immense.

Williams and Colomb explain that "as you begin a sentence, you have to prepare your reader for new and therefore important information." The proverb about the nail and the battle does that. It starts each new sentence with words that were in the previous sentence. It moves, quite systematically, from old to new information—which is a big reason why it is so easy to read and remember. Here it is again with the linked bits of language identified.

For want of a nail, the <u>shoe</u> was lost.
For want of a <u>shoe</u>, the <u>horse</u> was lost.
For want of a <u>horse</u>, the <u>knight</u> was lost.

For want of a <u>knight</u>, the battle was lost—
All for want of a nail.

Without these kinds of connections between sentences, your readers will get lost. They'll feel like your writing skips around too much, that it doesn't provide enough context for the ideas it introduces, that it's too choppy and scattered. Your words will seem more like a pile of disjointed notes than a coherent, well-constructed essay, email, or book.

On the other hand, if *all* you have is a connection between sentences—with no new information to keep readers interested—you'll have a different problem: your readers will get bored. Fast.

They'll get the sense that you're repeating yourself, that you are wasting their time, that you have run out of things to say. Who wants to read a sentence that says exactly what the previous sentence said? That's not writing. That's copying.

Venn Diagram

One way to visualize the move from old to new information is to imagine a Venn diagram. You want to avoid having two disconnected sentences, as is represented here:

Sentence 1   Sentence 2

What you want instead is some shared content. You want your sentences to overlap in a way that easily leads the reader from one to the other:

Sentence 1   Sentence 2

Oftentimes the overlap will come between the end of one sentence and the beginning of another. Williams and Colomb even go so far as to say that the "secret to clear and readable writing is in the first five or six words of every sentence." That's where you want to "locate your reader in familiar territory." It's a great place to quickly, almost seamlessly, orient their attention. Otherwise they might not get to the middle of the sentence, much less to the end.

Richard Rodriguez

It is possible, however, to structure your sentences a different way. You don't always have to put the overlapping content and language—what Williams and Colomb call the "old information"—in the beginning of the sentence. Skilled writers sometimes spread it throughout the sentences. A little in the beginning. A little in the middle. Maybe even some at the end.

Take a look at this passage from *Hunger of Memory*, Richard Rodriguez's account of his intellectual development as a Mexican American:

Of all the institutions in their lives, only the Catholic Church has seemed aware of the fact that my mother and father are thinkers—persons aware of the experience of their lives. Other institutions—the nation's political parties, the industries of mass entertainment and communications, the companies that employed them—have all treated my parents with condescension.

Now take a look at it again and notice where Rodriguez places the overlapping content and language. I've underlined it:

Of all the <u>institutions</u> in their lives, only the Catholic Church has seemed aware of the fact that <u>my mother and father</u> are thinkers—persons aware of the experience of their lives. Other <u>institutions</u>—the nation's political parties, the industries of mass entertainment and communications, the companies that employed them—have all treated <u>my parents</u> with condescension.

The word "institutions" from the first sentence shows up at the very beginning of the second sentence. But the phrase "my parents"—which references "my mother and father" in the first sentence—shows up more toward the end of the second sentence, after a long string of new information. That placement is fine, particularly if you are a more advanced writer, like Rodriguez. The important thing is that your content be mixed: readers need some old information, and they need some new information. An absence of either will cause serious problems.

Dumbo and Velcro

To get the proper mix, your sentences need to listen to each other. They need to pay attention to and expand on what came before, like a good dinner guest advancing the conversation. F. Scott Fitzgerald's sentences do this. Doris Kearns Goodwin's sentences do this. So do the sentences of W. E. B. Dubois, H. L. Mencken,

M. K. Fisher, and V. S. Naipaul. You could imagine the sentences of all these writers—and plenty of others—having big, attentive, Dumbo-like ears, ones that catch and catalog not just everything that has been said in a previous sentence but also everything that has been said in previous paragraphs, sections, and chapters. Skilled communicators know that to write well, you need to hear well. You need to hear what's around you; you need to hear what has come before you; and you certainly need to hear what you yourself have already shared.

You also need to lay a foundation for what will come next. Think of the old information parts of your sentences as layers of Velcro. Once that Velcro is firmly in place, the new information parts of your sentences will more easily stick.

Or think of it as some other kind of bridge, link, or common frame of reference: anything that helps prepare readers for fresh material. Readers often need this extra preparation. They need additional guidance and signposting.

You may know where your thoughts are headed—but they don't. It is impolite, even mean, to leave them stranded.

QUESTIONS SECTION

What can words do
but link what we know
to what we don't,
and so form a shape?

—Mark Doty, "Difference" (1983)

Clarity and Coherence: Questions*

(1) **Food:** Parents of picky eaters are often told to pair familiar foods with unfamiliar foods. If a five-year-old starts with something she is used to, perhaps she'll find it easier to try the newer item. You can think of that as an old information → new information move. Food companies are actually pretty systematic about this kind of move, as Michael Moss reveals in his Pulitzer Prize–winning book *Salt, Sugar, Fat*. Here is the account he gives of a conversation he had with an executive at Oscar Mayer who helped create one of the company's most famous products for kids:

> The testing [for the product], which went on for months, surpassed Oscar Mayer's highest hopes. Not only did the people in the experiment go for the [product's] trays after being exposed to the advertising, the familiarity of the contents, however plain they were, proved to be a foundational theorem in processed foods, which [the executive] calls "the weirdness factor": if a new product is too unusual, shoppers get scared. "I used the term '80% familiar,'" the executive told me. "If you've got a new thing, it better be 80% familiar, or you'll have people scratching their heads wondering what the hell it is."

---

* For answers, see page 230 of Appendix C.

Unscramble the letters to identify the famous product.

U L C N A L B E S H

(2) **Anadiplosis:** There is a term for the way writers (and speakers) take the same language that ended one sentence or clause and use it to begin the next sentence or clause. It's called "anadiplosis." You can think of it as a stylistically exaggerated form of going from old information to new information. Some examples of this move are below. Match them with their source (on the next page).

Examples
- "Having power makes [totalitarian leadership] isolated; isolation breeds insecurity; insecurity breeds suspicion and fear; suspicion and fear breed violence."
- "Meaning requires content, content requires time, time requires resistance."
- "If you didn't grow up like I did then you don't know, and if you don't know then it is probably better you don't judge."
- "Once you change your philosophy, you change your thought pattern. Once you change your thought pattern, you change your attitude. Once you change your attitude, it changes your behavior pattern and then you go on into some action. As long as you gotta sit-down philosophy, you'll have a sit-down thought pattern, and as long as you think that old sit-down thought, you'll be in some kind of sit-down action."
- "There are certain social principles in human nature from which we may draw the most solid conclusions with respect to the conduct of individuals and communities. We love our families more than our neighbors; we love our neighbors more than our countrymen in general."

Source

- Alexander Hamilton, "Constitutional Convention of New York" (1788)
- Zbigniew Brzezinski, *The Permanent Purge: Politics in Soviet Totalitarianism* (1956)
- Karl Ove Knausgaard, *My Struggle: Book 1* (2012)
- Junot Díaz, *The Brief Wondrous Life of Oscar Wao* (2007)
- Malcolm X, "The Ballot or the Bullet" (1964)

(3) **Kids:** Anadiplosis sometimes shows up in children's stories too. Identify the one word that fills in the blanks in each example. (The third example has three blank slots because the word that fills them is also included in the title of the source.)

"Right now, honey, the world just wants us to _____ in, and to _____ in we just gotta be like everybody else."

—*The Incredibles* (2004)

"If you don't eat, you'll be _____. If you are _____, you'll be slow; if you are slow, you'll die."

—*Kubo and the Two Strings* (2016)

"That buzzing noise means something. Now, the only reason for making a buzzing noise that I know of is because you are . . . a bee! And the only reason for being a bee is to make _____. And the only reason for making _____ is so I can eat it."

—A. A. Milne, *Winnie the Pooh and the _____ Tree* (1966)

(4) **Law:** Another way Joseph Williams and Gregory Colomb explain the principle of old information → new information in *Style: Toward Clarity and Grace* is by making an analogy to teachers:

> All of us recognize this principle when a good teacher tries to teach us something new. That teacher will always try to connect something we already know to whatever new information we are trying to learn.

Fill in the blanks below to modify the analogy to fit lawyers. You can use the word bank to help you. Imagine you are reading the passage from the perspective of a judge.

> All of us recognize this principle when a good _____ tries to teach us something new. That _____ will always try to connect some _____ we already _____ to whatever new _____ we are trying to _____.

Word Bank: case, lawyer, decided, lawyer, case, resolve

(5) **Movies:** Identify the movie based on the quote.

"They call for you: The general who became a slave; the slave who became a gladiator; the gladiator who defied an emperor. Striking story."
- (A) *The Patriot*
- (B) *Braveheart*
- (C) *The Rock*
- (D) *Gladiator*

"Fear is the path to the dark side. Fear leads to anger. Anger leads to hate. Hate leads to suffering."
- (A) *Star Wars: The Phantom Menace*
- (B) *Star Wars: The Force Awakens*
- (C) *Poltergeist*
- (D) *Poltergeist II: The Other Side*

"If we don't get this, we don't get the shot. If we don't get the shot, we don't get the movie. If we don't get the movie, we're all up the creek."
- (A) George Lucas to Steven Spielberg on the set of *Raiders of the Lost Ark*
- (B) Steven Spielberg to George Lucas on the set of *Raiders of the Lost Ark*
- (C) George Lucas to Steven Spielberg on the set of *Jurassic Park*
- (D) Steven Spielberg to George Lucas on the set of *Jurassic Park*

EXAMPLES SECTION

. . . a voice reciting in Japanese

Hi was Ri ni katazu

Ri wa ho ni katazu,

Ho wa Ken ni katazu

Ken wa Ten ni katazu

Which is the slogan of a Kamikaze unit, an Ohka outfit—it means:

Injustice cannot conquer Principle,

Principle cannot conquer Law,

Law cannot conquer Power,

Power cannot conquer Heaven.

—Thomas Pynchon, *Gravity's Rainbow* (1973)

Clarity and Coherence: Examples

(1) **Teaching:** "It is an odd circumstance that neither the old nor the new, by itself, is interesting: the absolutely old is insipid; the absolutely new makes no appeal at all. The old *in* the new is what claims the attention—the old with a slightly new turn. No one wants to hear a lecture on a subject completely disconnected with his previous knowledge, but we all like lectures on subjects of which we know a little already, just as, in the fashions, every year must bring its slight modification of last year's suit, but an abrupt jump from the fashion of one decade into another would be distasteful to the eye."

—William James, *Talk to Teachers on Psychology* (1899)

(2) **Psychology:** "Too novel and it's unfamiliar. Too familiar and it's boring. But in between and it's just right.

"When British psychologists examined how much people liked different last names, for example, they found just this pattern. Students were asked to consider sixty different surnames, randomly selected from the telephone directory. Half the students rated how much they liked the different last names, while the other half rated how familiar the names were. Very unfamiliar names, such as Baskin, Nall, and Bodle, weren't liked that much. At the other end of the spectrum, highly familiar names such as Smith and Brown were also disliked. So what did people like?

"Turns out the names people liked the most were the ones that fell in the middle. Names like Shelley or Cassel that were moderately familiar (at least to Brits). Right between unfamiliar and too familiar was just right.

"Familiarity and novelty can also be mixed in the same item. Some elements of a song (a chord progression or a singer's voice) may be familiar, while others (the lyrics) are new. A new recipe for turkey chili takes something you've made many times before (chili) and puts a novel spin on it. Just like similar sounding names, these variations on a theme increase liking."

—Jonah Berger, *Invisible Influence: The Hidden Forces That Shape Behavior* (2016)

(3) **Poverty:** "It sucks to be poor, and it sucks to feel that you somehow deserve to be poor. You start believing that you're poor because you're stupid and ugly. And then you start believing that you're stupid and ugly because you're Indian. And because you're Indian, you start believing that you're destined to be poor. It's an ugly circle and there's nothing you can do about it. Poverty doesn't give you strength or teach you lessons about perseverance. No, poverty only teaches you how to be poor."

—Sherman Alexie, *The Absolutely True Diary of a Part-Time Indian* (2007)

(4) **Hit Makers:** "This is the first thesis of the book. Most consumers are simultaneously neophilic—curious to discover new things—and

deeply neophobic—afraid of anything that's too new. The best hit makers are gifted at creating moments of meaning by marrying new and old, anxiety and understanding. They are architects of familiar surprises."

—Derek Thompson, *Hit Makers: The Science of Popularity in an Age of Distraction* (2017)

(5) **Kiran Desai:** "The more pampered you are the more pampered you will be the more presents you receive the more presents you will get the more presents you receive the more you are admired the more you will be admired the more you are admired the more presents you will get the more pampered you will be—"

—Kiran Desai, *The Inheritance of Loss* (2006)

(6) **Margaret Thatcher:** "Without a healthy economy, we can't have a healthy society; and without a healthy society, the economy won't stay healthy for long."

—Margaret Thatcher, "Speech to Conservative Party Conference" (1980)

(7) **Salman Rushdie:** "In the secret grassy quadrangle of the Gardens, I crawled before I could walk, I walked before I could run, I ran before I could dance, I danced before I could sing, and I danced and sang until I learned stillness and silence and stood motionless and listening at the Gardens' heart, on summer evenings sparkling with fireflies and became, at least in my own opinion, an artist . . . a would-be writer of films."

—Salman Rushdie, *The Golden House* (2017)

(8) **Shakespeare:** "My conscience hath a thousand several tongues / And every tongue brings in a several tale, / And every tale condemns me for a villain."

—William Shakespeare, *Richard III* (1597)

PRACTICE SECTION

"Second platoon," he says. "They're the tip of the spear. They're the main effort for the company, and the company is the main effort for the battalion, and the battalion is the main effort for the brigade. I put them down there against the enemy because I know they're going to get out there and they're not going to be afraid."

—Sebastian Junger, *War* (2010)

Practice Section: Old Friends

Background

In *The Art of Advocacy*, Noah Messing of Yale Law School uses a clever analogy to explain (1) the interplay between old information and new information and (2) why it is so often preferable to give some old information before you give any new information. He says that telling readers what they already know before you tell them something new is "the cognitive equivalent of what happens to most people when they walk into a crowded room. If they immediately see a few friends, they will calm down. But if they see a slew of unfamiliar faces, most people will be anxious and uncomfortable." He therefore offers this advice to lawyers and law students: "Your briefs and motions will make judges comfortable if your sentences greet them with old friends."

Assignment

Find the "old friends" in a piece of writing you admire. The piece could be from a novel. It could be from a memoir. It could be from an essay, contract, or letter. (If you are looking for letters, Martin Luther King's "Letter From Birmingham Jail" is a good candidate, as are any of the ones Warren Buffet has written to the shareholders of Berkshire Hathaway. Or you can browse the many great examples collected by Shaun Usher in his book and website *Letters of Note.*)

Once you find your piece, focus on four or five paragraphs. Circle or in some other way highlight any "old friend" you see as you move from sentence to sentence. Note the old friend's placement. Note its form: does it use the exact same word that appeared in a previous sentence? Does it use a close synonym? A pronoun?

Then take a look at four or five paragraphs of your own writing. How many old friends show up there? If there aren't enough to make the reader comfortable, add more to the party. If there are too many, kick some of the old friends out and make more room for new ones. They'll bring fresh insights and information with them.

Important Reminder: An old friend can be from more than just the previous sentence. It can also come from farther back in the paragraph or even from earlier paragraphs. It just has to be something your readers will recognize.

NINE

Good Sentences

Be a good steward of your gifts.
Protect your time. Feed your inner life.
Avoid too much noise. Read good books,
have good sentences in your ears.

—Jane Kenyon, "Notes for a Lecture: Everything
I Know About Writing Poetry" (1999)

Good Sentences: Concept

He is careful what he reads, for that is what he will write.
—Annie Dillard, *The Writing Life* (1989)

To write good sentences, you need to read good sentences. Skilled writers and editors know this, so they seek out good sentences wherever they can find them—the short stories of Alice Munro, the political essays of William F. Buckley, even well-crafted cartoons, speeches, and advertisements. They read not just with voracity but also with an eye toward larceny, always on the lookout for moves they can learn and repurpose.

In this way, skilled writers and editors combine two pieces of advice: one from Judge Frank Easterbrook, who is among the best judicial writers around, and one from Francine Prose, who is among the best literary writers around.

The advice from Judge Easterbrook comes from an interview in 2014. "Spend more time reading," Easterbrook said when asked what young lawyers could do to improve their writing skills. He specifically recommended the novels of Ernest Hemingway, William Faulkner, and Saul Bellow, though he also said much can be learned from regularly reading well-edited magazines like the *Atlantic* and *Commentary*. "The best way to become a good legal writer," he insisted, "is to spend more time reading good prose."

The advice from Francine Prose comes early in her 2006 book *Reading Like a Writer*. "Too often, students are being taught to read as if literature were some kind of ethics class or civics class—or worse, some kind of self-help manual. In fact, the important thing is the way the writer uses the language." She later notes that "every so often I'll hear writers say that there are other writers they would read if for no other reason than to marvel at the skill with which they can put together the sort of sentences that move us to read closely, to disassemble and reassemble them, much the way a mechanic might learn about an engine by taking it apart."

Embrace this craft-like approach to reading. Pay attention not just to a passage's content but to its composition, to how it was put together word by word, sentence by sentence. Study how paragraphs are constructed, how their various parts work together to communicate information clearly, effectively, and sometimes beautifully. Your writing will improve. Your rhythm will improve. Your readers will be grateful.

Ted Williams, Jimi Hendrix, and Édouard Manet

When baseball great Ted Williams joined the Boston Red Sox as a 21-year-old rookie in 1939, the best hitter on the team was a slugger named Jimmie Foxx. Williams idolized Foxx, who was so strong and imposing that Lefty Gomez, a star pitcher for the New York Yankees, once remarked that even Foxx's hair had muscles. Because Foxx drank buttermilk, Williams drank buttermilk—despite not liking the stuff at all. And because watching Foxx take batting practice before games gave Williams a chance to study the mechanics of a future Hall of Famer, Williams consistently carved out time to do so. "To play good baseball," Williams seemed to believe, "you need to watch good baseball."

Jimi Hendrix did something similar when he first started becoming serious about the guitar. In the early 1960s, well before he would redefine what it meant to play "The Star-Spangled Banner" and eventually become what the Rock & Roll Hall of Fame describes as "the most gifted instrumentalist of all time," Hendrix went on the "Chitlin Circuit," a collection of venues throughout the Southern, Eastern, and upper Midwestern parts of the United States that welcomed black performers during a period of intense segregation. Still only a backup musician, Hendrix used the time to learn as much as he could from legends like Otis Redding, Wilson Pickett, Little Richard, Solomon Burke, and the Isley Brothers.

Similar patterns of intense, imitative immersion in the work of others can be found in the career trajectories of musicians as different as the composer Joseph Haydn, the jazz virtuoso Charlie Parker, and the Queen of Soul, Aretha Franklin. "To make good music," they might all say, "you need to hear good music."

Visual artists are no different. In 1850, 18-year-old Édouard Manet, the future star of Impressionist painting, registered as a copyist at the Louvre Museum in Paris. He spent hours a day imitating the works of Renaissance greats like Titian, Tintoretto, and Domenico Ghirlandaio. "To paint good paintings," the lesson is, "you need to see good paintings—and maybe even copy them too."

Digital Library

Not everyone has access to the Louvre, as Manet did. Or to the legends of the Chitlin Circuit, as Jimi Hendrix did. And certainly nobody has access anymore to Jimmie Foxx, up close in a batting cage, as Ted Williams did. But everyone can have access to world-class writing, regardless of your field, age, or profession. Your local library and bookstore make that possible. So do Amazon, Project Gutenberg, and the online versions of well-edited magazines and newspapers. The University of Michigan Law School has even developed its own repository of excellent writing. Aware that many of the sentences students read for class come from convoluted statutes and clunkily composed judicial opinions, it has created a digital library designed to expose them to the patterns and techniques of passages that are much more elegant and engaging. The resource is called, straightforwardly enough, "Good Sentences" (http://libguides.law.umich.edu/goodsentences/home).

The Good Sentences library at Michigan is devoted to writing related to law. But you can imagine a Good Sentences library devoted to writing related to medicine, or engineering, or fashion, or physics, or anything really. You can imagine one set up for fifth graders, another set up for high schoolers, still another set up for each variety of graduate student: linguists, biologists, art historians, dentists. "Every discipline has a literature," William Zinsser explains in *Writing to Learn*, "a body of writing that students and teachers can use as a model; writing is learned mainly by imitation."

You might also imagine a Good Sentences library personally set up for yourself. Pick a subject. Find people who have written sentences you admire. And then read them, preferably out loud, preferably every day, preferably with an understanding that regardless of your career ambitions, much of your life will be spent composing sentences. You'll compose them at work. You'll compose them at home. You'll compose them on your computer and on your phone. You'll even compose them at least a few times, I hope, by hand—especially when you really want to make a personal connection.

Nobody is born knowing how to do this. But there are more than enough good sentences already written in the world to give you sufficient models to learn from, with plenty more being crafted each day, on every subject, and in countless mediums. If you read widely enough, if you read well enough, perhaps you'll even craft some yourself.

QUESTIONS SECTION

Can you imagine a musician who does not listen to music himself? The same question can be asked about writing. Every author writes for readers; no grammar rules and writing techniques will help you understand your reader if you do not read yourself.

—Mike Hanski, "Want to Be a Better Writer? Read More" (2017)

Good Sentences: Questions[*]

(1) **Founding Father:** One of America's most famous Founding Fathers recalls being told at a very young age that his writing "fell short in elegance of expression." Wanting to improve, he tried the following tactic: he studied the sentences in a well-edited periodical called the *Spectator* and then attempted to produce those sentences himself. A fuller description of his approach appears in his autobiography, which started out as an extended letter to one of his sons. He hoped to pass on the important lessons and habits of his life. Here is a sample.

> I bought [the *Spectator*], read it over and over, and was much delighted with it. I thought the writing excellent, and wished, if possible, to imitate it. With this view, I took some of the papers, and, making short hints of the sentiment in each sentence, laid them by a few days, and then, without looking at the book, try'd to complete the papers again, by expressing each hinted sentiment at length, and as fully as it had been expressed before, in any suitable words that should come to hand. Then I compared my *Spectator* with the original, discovered some of my faults,

---

[*] For answers, see page 233 of Appendix C.

and corrected them.... By comparing my work afterwards with the original, I discovered many faults and amended them; but I sometimes had the pleasure of fancying that, in certain particulars of small import, I had been lucky enough to improve the method of the language, and this encouraged me to think I might possibly in time come to be a tolerable English writer, of which I was extremely ambitious.

Identify the Founding Father.
   (A) Thomas Jefferson
   (B) Benjamin Franklin
   (C) Woodrow Wilson
   (D) James Madison
   (E) Theodore Roosevelt

(2) **Founding Mother:** One of America's most famous Founding Mothers also spent a lot of time reading the *Spectator*. Here are some other things she read, according to a biography by Stanford's Edith Gelles that uses the phrase "A Writing Life" as its subtitle.

- Shakespeare
- the English poets Alexander Pope and William Cowper
- local newspapers
- medical tracts
- the Bible
- the French playwright Molière
- works of history and political theory in her husband's library

Identify the Founding Mother.
   (A) Jane Franklin
   (B) Sally Hemings
   (C) Abigail Adams
   (D) Martha Washington
   (E) Dolly Madison

[Hint: She gave the following famous instruction to her husband in March of 1776, when he and the rest of the Continental Congress were trying to rewrite the laws of the nation: "Remember the Ladies, and be more generous and favorable to them than your ancestors."]

(3) **Cartoons:** For twenty years, Bob Mankoff was the cartoon editor at *The New Yorker*, widely considered the preeminent place
to publish humorous drawings. His path there wasn't inevitable.
Still a freelance artist back in the late 1970s, he submitted 2,000
cartoons to the magazine before even one was accepted. What
seemed to make a difference, what seemed to help push Mankoff's drawings out of the rejection pile and into the pages of
magazine, was the time he spent studying previously published
cartoons. Here's how he describes his approach:

> Determined to educate myself on what a *New Yorker* car-
> toon was, and what mine weren't, I took myself off to the
> New York Public Library. There, the collected volumes of
> *The New Yorker* included every issue, and therefore every
> cartoon, published up until that time. I planned to look
> at all of them.

This description appears in a book Mankoff titled after his most
famous cartoon. It shows a man talking on the phone in his
impressive-looking office. The man has a suit on. He has a big
window behind him with a great view of the city. And he is flipping through what appears to be a day planner or calendar as the
person on the other line futilely tries to schedule a meeting with
him. "No, Thursday's no good—" the man says in the first half of
the caption. Guess what he says in the second half?

"How about ___? Does ____ work for you?"
- (A) next week
- (B) when the cows come home
- (C) when pigs fly
- (D) never

(4) **Retail:** Early on in his career, the founder of one of the largest companies in the world used a Good Sentences approach to learn what makes a business in his industry successful—although instead of reading lots of sentences, he visited lots of stores. Below is an account of those visits. It comes from his 2012 autobiography *Made in America*:

> I began to hear talk of the early discounters—companies like Ann & Hope, whose founder, Marty Chase, is generally considered the father of discounting. Spartan's and Mammoth Mart and Two Guys From Harrison and Zayre and Arlan's were all starting up in the Northeast, and I remembered that lesson I'd learned a long time ago in Newport with the panties selling in such huge volume when they were priced at $1, instead of $1.20. So I started running all over the country, studying the concept from the mill stores in the East to California, where Sol Price started his Fed-Mart in 1955. I guess I've stolen—I actually prefer the word "borrowed"—as many ideas from Sol Price as from anybody else in the business.

Name the company this person eventually started.

(A) Kmart
(B) Gap
(C) Sam's Wholesale
(D) Walmart

(5) **Soccer:** "If there is a [soccer] game on, take some time to watch it. . . . If you are flipping through channels and stumble upon a game, watch it for a while. Get to know the players, their styles, and their teams. If you want to be a good player, it's not a bad investment of your time. And if your parents give you grief, tell them I said soccer is educational TV."

This advice appeared in the memoir *Go for the Goal: A Champion's Guide to Winning in Soccer and Life.* Unscramble the letters to identify the author.

First Name: I A M
Last Name: M A H M

EXAMPLES SECTION

If you don't have the time to read, you don't have the time (or tools) to write. Simple as that.

—Stephen King, *On Writing* (1999)

Good Sentences: Examples

(1) **Joyce Carol Oates:** "Young or beginning writers must be told to read widely, ceaselessly."

—Joyce Carol Oates, *The Faith of a Writer: Life, Craft, Art* (2003)

(2) **Chief Justice John Roberts:** "I've always said the only way to be a good writer is to be a good reader. You can't do it consciously. You can't say, 'This is how you need to structure a sentence.' But your mind structures the words and it sees them, and when you try to write them again, they tend to come out better because your mind is thinking of what was a pleasing sentence to read and remembers that when you try to write."

—Chief Justice John Roberts, "Bryan Garner: Interviews with Supreme Court Justices" in *Scribes Journal of Legal Writing* (2010)

(3) **Jhumpa Lahiri:** "Writing comes from reading."

—Jhumpa Lahiri, *In Other Words* (2016)

(4) **Professor X:** "I have come to think that the twist ingredients in the mysterious mix that makes a good writer may be (1) having read enough throughout a lifetime to have internalized the rhythms of the written word, and (2) refining the ability to mimic those rhythms."

—Professor X, *In the Basement of the Ivory Tower: Confessions of an Accidental Academic* (1994)

(5) **William Zinsser:** "If anyone asked me how I learned to write, I'd say I learned by reading the men and women who were doing the kind of writing I wanted to do and trying to figure out how they did it."

—William Zinsser, *Writing to Learn* (1993)

(6) **Judge Henry Friendly:** "Remarkably, in addition to serving his [Supreme Court] Justice well, during the year's clerkship Friendly appears to have read most of the decisions ever rendered by the Supreme Court."

—David Dorsen, *Henry Friendly, Greatest Judge of His Era* (2012)

(7) **Michael Chabon:** "I just copied the writers whose voices I was responding to, and I think that's probably the best way to learn."

—Michael Chabon, quoted by Christopher Taylor in an interview in *The Guardian* (2010)

(8) **Deliberate Practice:** "First, identify the expert performers, then figure out what they do that makes them so good, then come up with training techniques that allow you to do it, too."

—Anders Ericsson and Robert Pool, *Peak: Secrets From the New Science of Expertise* (2016)

PRACTICE SECTION

Read widely and with discrimination. Bad writing is contagious.
—P. D. James, "Ten Rules for Writing Fiction" (2010)

Practice Section #1: Reading List for Life

Background

One way to think about college is that it gives you a reading list for life. This seems particularly true for students who take humanities classes, but a similar approach could work for students whose subject area of choice is different. Chemistry, physics, engineering, economics, math—there are great, readable books in every field. So don't waste your time slogging through bad or even mediocre writing. There is too much great stuff out there to settle for anything that isn't at once enjoyable and enlightening.

Assignment

Part A

Think of some of your favorite teachers in college—or even back in high school. What books did they put on their syllabus? What did they recommend you spend your time reading?

Depending on when you graduated, perhaps some of your teachers are still active and have posted syllabi and book recommendations online. Even if they haven't, I imagine many of them would appreciate a note from you saying (1) you still think of their classes and (2) you would love to hear about what they are reading now. So carve out some time in the next week to write one of them an email—better yet, handwrite a letter. You'll likely brighten their day, and you may even end up with your next great read.

Part B

If you weren't lucky enough to have good teachers—or don't feel comfortable reaching out to any—there are plenty of public curators you can turn to for reading recommendations. Lists of "Best Books of the Year" usually find their way into both print and online publications; prize committees like the Pulitzer and the National Book Award generally don't select rubbish, and many prominent people—from Bill Gates to Oprah Winfrey—do a lot of sorting and selecting for you by sharing their recent reading picks.

But start small. Focus on three or four sources of recommendations for now. Otherwise the whole process might get overwhelming, even paralyzing. All you are looking for are two books you will definitely read in the next year. You can graduate to more ambitious goals later.

Another thing to keep in mind: Don't rush through the books. Take your time. Try to savor them. This isn't fast food snatched from a drive-through window; this is slow food expertly prepared by chefs who cook with only the highest quality of ingredients. Said differently, the selection criteria you apply should be: "Reading these sentences will be good for my brain—and eventually, my pen."

Bottom Line: If you want more professional and elegant outputs, you need to be very deliberate about your inputs.

* * *

Here are some combinations of lists you might consider:

Combination #1

New York Times: Notable Books of the Year
Financial Times: The Best Business Books of All Time
BBC: The 21st Century's 12 Greatest Novels

Combination #2

Discover Magazine: 25 Best Science Books of All Time
Cosmopolitan: 20 Political Books Every Woman Should Read
National Review: 100 Best Non-Fiction Books of the Century

Combination #3

Sports Illustrated: Top 100 Sports Books of All Time
Rolling Stone: 10 Best Music Books
Amazon: 100 Biographies and Memoirs to Read in a Lifetime

Combination #4

National Endowment for the Arts: The Big Read
ABA Journal: 30 Lawyers, 30 Books
Independent: 10 Best Short Story Collections

Practice Section #2: Hand–Arm–Head

Background

Bruce Edwards has been a math professor at the University of Florida for more than four decades. The winner of many teaching awards, he has a great way of capturing why it is important to build in time for more active forms of learning, even to the point of creating muscle memory. A lot of learning, he says, enters through your hand, travels up your arm, and only then lodges in your brain. You don't master calculus by simply reading books on integrals and listening to lectures on logarithms; you master calculus by taking out a piece of paper and actually doing calculus problems.

A similar thing can be said about writing. To really improve as a writer, you need to go through the physical act of constructing sentences. Reading and listening to them isn't enough.

Assignment

Combine the idea of Good Sentences with the Hand–Arm–Head approach Edwards describes. Pick a passage from your favorite book, blog, brief, speech, poem, or magazine. Then handwrite it slowly, word by word, sentence by sentence.

Pretend you're the one composing the passage. Pretend you're choosing each phrase and clause. Then ask yourself these kinds of questions:

- Why are you going to pick this verb instead of a different verb?
- Why are you going to end the paragraph where you do?
- What is the function of the second sentence?
  - How will it set up the third?
- What is the reason behind each punctuation mark?
  - Do any purposefully deviate from the conventions of grammar?
  - Do any need to be revised?
- How particular are you going to be?
- Where do you show restraint?

There is a scene in the 2000 movie *Finding Forrester* directed by Gus Van Sant that involves a similar exercise. A reclusive novelist played by Sean Connery begins to mentor, albeit very reluctantly, an inner-city teen who has a surplus of literary ambition but a real lack of literary skills. Seeing at one point that the teen is battling a particularly bad case of writer's block, Connery's character takes out a story he himself had written several decades ago. He gives it to the teen and says, "Start typing that. Sometimes the simple rhythm of typing gets us from page one to page two. And when you begin to feel your own words, start typing them."

* * *

If you decide to do this exercise on a computer, try to pick a passage that will fill up a whole page; if you stick to writing by hand, pick one that will only fill up half a page. Either way, think about the connections between the words you're reproducing, the way they fit together to create a coherent, rhythmic whole. You'll eventually want that to be true of your own writing.

TEN

To Name Is to Know and Remember

*I could no longer model the behavior
and trust that people would understand
and do it. I had to start naming stuff.*

—restauranteur Danny Meyer, quoted by
Daniel Coyle in *The Talent Code* (2009)

To Name Is to Know and Remember: Concept

Once it has a name, I can fix it.

> —Nora Ephron, "My Aruba," in *I Remember Nothing* (2010)

In the late [1980s], SportsCenter was an hour show on Sunday, the only SportsCenter that was an hour long. One week, I had a hold in the show that was about seven minutes long, because it was the British Open and we just had that and baseball. So I said, "Let's have Cliff Drysdale interview Jack Nicklaus, and talk to him about anything besides the British Open. I don't care about the British Open, I just want to talk to him about the state of golf." And the interview was really good. He talked about the state of the game and where he thought golf was going in the future. I called it "the Sunday Conversation," because I think you ought to title everything so it resonates with the viewer.

> —coordinating producer at ESPN, quoted by James
> Andrew Miller and Tom Shales in *Those Guys Have
> All the Fun: Inside the World of ESPN* (2011)

It is a lot easier to learn and remember something when it has a name. The biologist E. O. Wilson makes this point well in his 2002 book *The Future of Life*. "The beginning of every science is the description of phenomena," he writes. "We cannot think clearly about a plant or animal until we have a name for it; hence the pleasure of bird watching with a field guide in hand." The philosopher Susanne Langer gets at a similar idea in *Philosophy in a New Key*, a book that examines the power of symbols and language. In her view, "the notion of giving something a name is the vastest generative idea that ever was conceived."

But perhaps the best observations about this kind of naming, the kind that activates learning and memory, comes from Dana Gioia, a poet with a credential few other poets can match: an MBA from Stanford. In 2015, Gioia became the Poet Laureate of California. Seven years earlier, President George W. Bush awarded him the

President's Citizens Award for "his dedication to fostering creativity and expression and for helping preserve America's rich artistic legacy." In presenting the award, President Bush noted not just Gioia's achievements as a poet but also his productive tenure as head of the National Endowment of the Arts from 2003 to 2009. "He has advanced some of our most treasured traditions, expanded public support for the arts and arts education, and increased the understanding and appreciation of the arts among our nation's youth," Bush said.

Before doing all that, however, Gioia spent fifteen years at General Foods, which merged with Kraft in 1990 to form one of the largest food and beverage companies in the world. Gioia rose to the level of vice president at General Foods and helped developed some of its best-known brands, including Kool-Aid and Jell-O. One of his biggest successes was the creation of "Jell-O Jigglers." It's not hard to imagine Gioia's skill with language played some role in the product's alliterative marketing.

Words

This skill is on full display in "Words," the poem in which Gioia offers his observations about the power of naming.* First published in an award-winning collection called *Interrogations at Noon*, the poem starts out by questioning the value of words themselves. Here's how it opens:

> *The world does not need words. It articulates itself*
> *in sunlight, leaves, and shadows.*

It then notes that earthly phenomena do not wait around for us to classify and measure them. Their existence does not depend on any

---

* Gioia has generously made the whole poem available on his website: http://danagioia.com/words/.

abstract label or name. "The stones on the path / are no less real for lying uncatalogued and uncounted" is how Gioia puts it. "The fluent leaves speak only the dialect of pure being."

The first time I read the phrase "the dialect of pure being" I was a bit put off. It sounded like something you might see above the door of a bad yoga studio: "In here, we speak only the dialect of pure being."

But the more I reread the phrase—and reread the lines nearby—the more I started to nod in agreement. Perhaps we overvalue words, the lines suggest. Perhaps they're not as important as we think. Perhaps they can even have a corrupting effect, ruinously turning a seemingly wonderful experience like a kiss into "something less or other."

> The kiss is fully itself though no words were spoken.
>
> And one word transforms it into something less or other—
> *illicit, chaste, perfunctory, conjugal, covert.*

Before words, the "kiss" Gioia describes was just a kiss. But now, because of their meddling influence, the kiss is an "illicit kiss" or a "perfunctory kiss" or a "covert kiss." Now the kiss has been sullied.

This doesn't mean that words are bad, of course. But sometimes they can tarnish what they touch. Other times, they're just plain inadequate, as many have discovered when trying to console a friend, express appreciation, or communicate disappointment.

Yet what is so great about Gioia's poem, at least for our purposes, is that at the same time that the poem acknowledges the limits of words, it also celebrates, in a later stanza, their pedagogical power, their ability to teach us something about the world that, without them, we wouldn't understand or even notice.

Gioia uses stones as an example. If you don't know the names of specific stones, he explains, if you don't have a vocabulary to help you identify key differences in color and composition, your understanding of them will stay pretty limited.

Yet the stones remain less real to those who cannot
name them, or read the mute syllables graven in silica.
To see a red stone is less than seeing it as jasper—
metamorphic quartz, cousin to the flint the Kiowa
carved as arrowheads.

Gioia sums up this idea with a wonderful phrase: "To name is to know and remember." It's worth repeating, particularly if you are at all involved in education, either as a student or as a teacher: "To name is to know and remember."

To name something a "sunk cost," for example, is to know and remember an important concept in economics. Just like to name something "the Renaissance" is to know and remember an important period in history. Terms like "rectangle," "preposition," "Krebs cycle"—these all help fill in the basic contours of knowledge. They make learning possible.

Without them, without words, leaves may still speak the dialect of pure being, but our ability to describe and understand our world would be severely hampered.

The Coerver Method

"To name is to know and remember" is also the approach we have taken in this book. Concept by concept, we have developed a vocabulary I hope you can use to both identify and produce effective writing. Naming the concepts has been a big part of that process.

In this way, we have followed the lead not just of Gioia but also of the legendary Dutch soccer coach Wiel Coerver. In the 1970s, Coerver developed a very systematic, almost academic, approach to teaching soccer skills. He watched footage of the best players in the world. He dissected their play down into discrete moves. And then he had his own players practice those moves over and over again.

Greatness is teachable, Coerver believed. Brilliance can be learned. Skill and creativity are not necessarily innate.

If you played soccer growing up or have kids who do now, there is a good chance you have at some point met a coach who used the "Coerver method." I certainly remember being taught and then drilled on Coerver moves when I started playing. There was the "Revelino," the "Matthews," and, a personal favorite, the "Van Basten."

Other sports follow similar approaches to training and instruction. High jumpers learn the "Fosbury Flop." Wrestlers learn the "Karelin Lift." Figure skaters master a wide range of "axels"—from the single axel, to the double axel, to, if you are really good, the triple axel.

All of these techniques are named after the athletes who pioneered them. The Fosbury Flop is named after Dick Fosbury, who used it to win a gold medal at the 1968 Summer Olympics. The Karelin Lift is named after Aleksandr Karelin, who dominated Greco-Roman wrestling for much of the 1980s and 1990s, earning three Olympic gold medals and winning 888 of his 890 official matches. As for the "axel" in figure skating, that is named after Axel Paulsen. Back in 1882, he became the first skater to perform a forward jump.

What's nice about all the names is that they are at once efficient and precise, as are the ones Coerver picked when thinking up ways to help players develop better soccer skills. Take the "Cruyff Turn." Coerver named it after the great Dutch midfielder Johan Cruyff, who is widely considered to be one of the top five soccer players of all time. The move involves faking like you are going in one direction and then tucking the ball behind your opposite heel as you quickly head in the other direction. When done properly, it is both elegant and effective.

But imagine if every time you wanted a player to perform it, you had to say, "Chris, do the thing where you fake like you are going in one direction and then tuck the ball behind your opposite heel as you quickly head in the other direction." That's not going to be very helpful, for you or for Chris. Much easier, for everybody, would be if you could simply say, "Chris, do the Cruyff Turn." Or even, "Chis, do the Cruyff." The name gives coaches and players a way to communicate, store, and retrieve a lot of information. It's a tidy pedagogical package.

Writing, I think, can work the same way.

* * *

I'm not alone. The book *Point Made* by Ross Guberman names moves that top attorneys use to craft first-class motions and briefs. The book *They Say, I Say* by Cathy Birkenstein and Gerald Graff names moves that top academics use to craft first-class essays and research papers. And countless style guides proceed, if not exactly by naming moves, at least by identifying the component parts of sentences and paragraphs they think are worth emulating. It is a form of literary botany.

My preference is to borrow already-existing names (or concepts) and then adapt and supplement them as needed. The chapters of this book reflect that preference. I didn't come up with the idea of the "Words Under the Words." Naomi Shihab Nye did. Nor did I come up with the idea of grammar's "Infinite Power." Joan Didion did. I simply used these ideas to address common writing issues students, lawyers, and other writers face. The same is true of the "Rule of Three," "Sound and Sense," and "Corresponding Ideas in Corresponding Forms."

When I teach undergraduates, I'll often be a bit more adventurous: I'll actually make up new names for writing moves I want them to learn and try. There are usually formal labels for these moves already, but I have found that many students have trouble remembering them. Terms like "polysyndeton" and "anadiplosis" don't exactly roll off the tongue or stick in the mind. So in the two main courses I taught— "The Syntax of Sports" and "The Syntax of Slavery"—I tried to do a little better job marketing the English language.

I also gave the students in those courses some "Words to Write By." These are bits of advice that first began as scribblings on a chalkboard in Haven Hall, which is where many undergraduates at the University of Michigan go each day for class. I taught a section of 18 mostly first-year students. All seemed to appreciate when the day's writing lesson could be distilled into a tidy principle. One of the first principles turned out to be among the most fundamental: "Try to write something you would actually want to read."

I told the students that this principle applies not only to the short papers they had to hand in each week but also to all the other writing they would do, both in college and after. Emails, lab reports, application essays, thank-you notes—all of these would be greatly improved if they took some time to think about what it might feel like to be on the other end of their sentences and paragraphs.

I now make this point to law students by invoking the words of Ilse Crawford, whose renowned, London-based design firm Studioilse has worked on everything from upscale hotels to private homes to a product line at Ikea. "Empathy," Crawford says, "is the cornerstone of design." The first step is to imagine how the end user will interact with and respond to whatever you're creating. Said differently: it's not about you—it's about them.

For law students, this means thinking about what it might feel like to be the judge that reads their brief or the parties whose relationship will be dictated by the words and phrases of a particular contract. It means thinking of your writing as a product and making it as user-friendly as possible. Empathy helps with that.

So do, I hope, at least some of the following "Words to Write By." Previous students have found them useful. With any luck, you will too.

Words to Write By

When faced with writer's block: "Writing often comes down to having a conversation on the page. But sometimes that conversation first needs to happen with another person. So talk to people about what you are writing. Then, with their permission, scribble the best bits down on paper."

When stating the thesis of your paper or proposal: "If nobody would disagree with you, you're probably not saying anything that interesting."

When trying to come up with a new idea: "The key to coming up with a new idea is to make it not that new. So search around for things you already know and for things other people already know. A lot of innovation comes from recombination."

When wondering how to have long-term success as a writer: "Write. Every. Day."

When deciding whether to use a comma, dash, semicolon, or other punctuation mark: "Check the other punctuation you have already used in the sentence (or in surrounding sentences) before making your final decision. Punctuation affects other punctuation."

When deciding when to begin writing: "Toward the end of the project, as the deadline looms, you are probably going to want an extra day, week, or even month to finish. Take that time now, by starting earlier than you originally planned. Your future self will thank you—maybe even with a leisurely nap."

When trying to study or learn something: "Learning is not about having a photographic memory. It's about taking the right kind of pictures."

When considering whether to take on an ambitious project: "Trying is cool."

When things don't go as you hoped: "Failure is a public good. So share your mistakes with people. You'll help them learn, and you might even teach yourself something along the way."

When deciding where to go on spring break or some other vacation: "Try to visit, once a year if you can, a country less prosperous than your own."

When considering whether to take a trip overseas: "International travel: sounds great, feels terrible, usually worth it."

When giving feedback: "Remember: Few people like to be corrected. Most people prefer to be helped."

When frustrated by the process of writing: "Writing is rarely easy, but there are ways to make it less hard. Find a teacher who knows some of those ways—and then take *every* class they offer."

When mapping out the schedule for a long project: "Build in small wins. You need to remember what accomplishment feels like."

When editing: "Before handing something in, try to have at least one other set of eyes look it over. Your set is not to be trusted."

When trying to network: "A good way to network is to do excellent work. Then people will network for you."

When deciding when to network: "A good time to network is similar to a good time to negotiate: when you don't have to. Desperation is rarely attractive."

When deciding whether to spend some time learning how to write better: "The inability to write well is not a moral failing. But it can be a professional liability."

When picking classes: "Once you've paid tuition, learning to write in school is a lot less expensive than learning to write on the job. So take some writing classes before you graduate. And if you can't find any good ones, create your own. That's why the world invented the term 'independent study.'"

When about to use an unnecessarily fancy word or phrase or theory: "Trying to sound smart is a pretty dumb strategy. Writing is about connecting with people—not trying to impress them."

When thinking about your career: "Starting with what you like to do and then trying to figure out if there is some way you can get paid to do it seems like a much better strategy than starting with what you can get paid to do and then trying to figure out if there is some way you can like it."

When thinking about your current academic or professional circumstances: "How much of your day is spent doing things that make you smile with people who make you smile?"

When deciding what to feed your brain: "To write good sentences, you need to read good sentences. Be deliberate about your inputs."

When you feel like you are not getting anywhere on a piece of writing: "Trust the process—but every once in a while, have someone evaluate that process."

When you think you have finished a piece of writing: "Spend some extra time cleaning up your sentences. Your readers will be grateful."

When approaching the next few weeks of your life: "If you are going through hell, keep going. If you are going through heaven, sit for a while."

When approaching the next several decades of your life: "Embrace getting older. It just means you have more ages and experiences in your repertoire."

When meeting new folks, especially powerful folks: "Respect people's résumés. But do not be intimidated by them. They probably have a pretty big antirésumé as well. We all do."

When contemplating a career: "Beware of jobs where the principal use of your education is to exploit someone else's lack of education."

When engaged in a serious conflict: "An 'us against the world' mentality can be helpful—unless the world is right."

When making many kinds of decisions: "It is good to trust your instincts. It is better to trust your instincts when those instincts are informed by experience and education."

When thinking about your education: "The most important things you write in your life will probably not be in school. But what you learn in school can help you write those important things better."

APPENDIX A

SELF-ASSESSMENT

[Note: I give the assignment below to students at the beginning of the semester. But it works as a helpful exercise at other times as well, even if you are not on an academic calendar.]

This assignment is designed solely to help you and me figure out where you are as a writer now and where you would like to be as a writer by the end of the semester. With that goal in mind, please write one or two single-spaced pages that will accomplish several tasks:

(1) Tell a little bit about yourself as a writer.
   a. This part of your Self-Assessment might include past writing experiences, whether pleasant or unpleasant, rewarding or frightening—or some combination of all four. It might also describe what you go through as you are preparing to write and as you are actually writing:
   - Do you start with an outline?
   - Do you end by reading what you have written out loud?
   - Do you do your best writing in the library?
     - At home?
     - In the morning?
     - At night?

- Do you have no idea where or when you do your best writing because you kind of just write whenever you have to and usually only because a deadline is fast approaching?

  (If this last question describes you as a writer, don't worry: plenty of great writers would not be great writers without deadlines, real and imagined.)

b. Finally, this part of the assessment might address the different kinds of writing you have done in law school, before law school, or perhaps while contemplating doing something other than law school.

- When, for example, was the last time you wrote something that you yourself actually wanted to read?
- What conditions helped you produce that piece of writing?
- What obstacles, in your mind, prevent you from producing something like that again given your current schedule, habits, and level of preparation?

(2) Share some of your strengths and weaknesses as a writer.

a. What do you think you do well as a writer?

b. What do you think needs work?

This discussion can include not just an analysis of your finished product but other aspects of the writing process as well, such as getting through a first draft, editing down a final draft, or simply procrastinating to the point where you have written more words on Twitter in the past hour than you have on whatever project you're supposed to be working on.

(3) Conclude by identifying two goals for yourself as a writer this semester.

a. The first goal should be a "S.M.A.R.T." goal:

- Specific
- Measurable
- Achievable
- Relevant
- Time-bound

Your S.M.A.R.T. goal could be something like trying out a good writerly habit for, say, the next 30 days. Here are some examples of habits my students have picked. (Their check-in date is usually halfway through the semester.)

1. **Carry a notepad with me wherever I go and jot down ideas when they come to me.**

   An electronic version of this goal can be fulfilled with the "Notes" function on an iPhone or similar device. But I encourage using a physical pad because something magical often happens when you take the time to put pen to paper. Your mind slows. Your thoughts crystallize. You might just produce a second idea by the time you write down the first.

2. **Draft in one place. Edit in another.**

   The geographical distance between these two places need not be massive. Draft in your apartment. Edit in the library. Draft in your bedroom. Edit in your living room. The point is to separate the sometimes chaotic outpouring of ideas that is drafting from the necessarily careful shaping of ideas that is editing. You do not want to edit a piece of writing through the eyes of the person who drafted it. Instead, you want to edit it through the eyes of what the novelist Zadie Smith calls a "smart stranger." Geographic distance, however minimal, helps you become that.

3. **Call a friend or sibling or parent during each writing assignment and try to explain to them what I've already written and what I still have left to write.**

   Writing often comes down to having a conversation on a page. Only, first, that conversation usually needs to happen with another person. So talk to people about what you are writing—and then thank them profusely.

b. The second goal should be a "Stretch" goal: a more ambitious goal that, even if you don't fully achieve, could lead to some beneficial outcomes and discoveries. Here is how a 2017 article in the *Harvard Business Review* described the two key characteristics:

1. **Extreme difficulty**

   "Stretch goals involve radical expectations that go beyond current capabilities and performance. Consider Southwest Airlines' early stretch goal of achieving a 10-minute turnaround at airport gates. A familiar task was involved, but the target was a drastic departure from the industry standard at the time, which was close to one hour."

2. **Extreme novelty**

   "Brand-new paths and approaches must be found to bring a stretch goal within reach. In other words, working differently, not simply working harder, is required. To get gate turnarounds down to 10 minutes, Southwest had to completely overhaul its staff's work practices and reimagine the behavior of customers. The airline did, however, famously figure out how to reach this goal."

Stretch goals are not for everyone. And they are certainly not for everyone during law school. But for the purposes of this exercise, assume that a stretch goal *is* appropriate for you right now. What would you pick? What is something that is extremely difficult and extremely novel that you'd love to try to pull off by the time you graduate—or even by the end of the year or semester?

Here is a list to help trigger some ideas. Michigan students have done each of them. (Don't let that fact make you think pursuing something similar wouldn't be novel enough. The novelty would be in the change you would have to make to your current way of operating—not in the originality of the goal.)

- publish an op-ed in a Pulitzer Prize–winning newspaper
- start a business

- create a new student organization
- get a Skadden or Equal Justice Works fellowship
- win a national writing competition
- win a national moot court competition

[<u>Note</u>: Becoming a better writer would help with each of these goals.]

APPENDIX B

SELF-ASSESSMENT → SELF-RECOMMENDATION

[Note: This assignment is given to students halfway through the semester.]

Step 1: Identify one of the following:
- an organization or person you want to work for
- a program or school you would like to attend
- a fellowship, grant, or award you would like to win

Step 2: Read the Self-Assessment you wrote back at the beginning of the semester.

Step 3: Think hard about your performance in the course so far.
- Have you met the S.M.A.R.T. goal you set for yourself?
- Have you taken steps to pursue the Stretch Goal you set for yourself?
- Do you reliably meet deadlines?
- Can you (and your phone) be trusted to act in a respectful way during meetings?
- If you have asked for extensions or the chance to miss class, have you done so with sufficient notice and respect?
- Do you add value to classroom discussion, especially when it comes to helping people improve their writing? (A good data point is the résumé workshops we do.)

- How well have you juggled the expectations of this course with other demands on your time?

Step 4: Think hard about your current writing ability.

Mechanics

- Will readers find grammatical mistakes in your writing?
- Will readers have a hard time getting through your sentences, either because they are too long or because they are monotonously short?
- What is the ratio of concrete nouns to abstract nouns in your writing?
- Do you punctuate like a professional?

Organization

- Do your sentences flow nicely into each other?
- Do your paragraphs flow nicely into each other?
- Do your headings, sections, or chapters make logical sense—not just individually but when taken together?

Concepts

- How well do you use the "words under the words"?
- How well do you use the "infinite power of grammar"?
- How well do you use the "rule of three"?
- How well do you use the "power of the particular"?
- Are you often "uselessly accurate"?

Development

- Do you make use of an "extra ear"?
- Do you read your own work out loud?
- Is there evidence that you are getting better?
- Is there evidence that you are getting better at *getting better*?

Extenuating Circumstances

- Have you had to deal with circumstances that have made it particularly difficult for you to perform at your best this semester?

- What evidence can you provide that you'd perform better under different circumstances?

Step 5: Pretend you are me. Write a recommendation letter about yourself to whatever or whomever you identified in Step 1. Most recommendation letters are one to two pages long. If you end up writing three pages, that's fine. But don't go beyond that. Part of this exercise involves making difficult choices about what to highlight and what to leave out.

APPENDIX C

ANSWERS TO QUESTION SECTIONS

CHAPTER 1: THE WORDS UNDER THE WORDS

(1) **Legislation:** For more examples of rhetorical framing in politics—"drilling for oil vs. exploring for oil" and "tax cuts vs. tax relief"—read the essay "The Alchemy of a Political Slogan" by Alex Williams. It is in the August 22, 2004 issue of the *New York Times*.

(2) **Family Law:** More decision-makers gave the child to Parent B when the question was "To which parent would you award sole custody?" (36% awarded custody to Parent A vs. 64% awarded custody to Parent B). More decision-makers gave the child to Parent A when the question was "To which parent would you deny custody?" (45% denied custody to Parent A vs. 55% denied custody to Parent B).

(3) **Business:**

Company	Term
Trader Joe's	Crew Members
Disney Theme Parks	Cast Members/Imagineers
Starbucks	Baristas
Walmart	Associates
Apple	Geniuses/Creatives
Taco Bell	Food Champions

(4) **Human Trafficking:** For a discussion of the framing issues involved, see Liz Kelly, Surviving Sexual Violence 163–165 (Cambridge: Polity Press, 1988); Tami Spry, *In the Absence of Word and Body: Hegemonic Implications of "Victim" and "Survivor" in Women's Narratives of Sexual Violence*, 13.2 Women and Language 27 (1995); Stacy L. Young & Katheryn C. Maguire, *Talking About Sexual Violence*, 26.2 Women and Language 40–52 (2003).

(5) **Education:** (C) field lessons. Jay Mathews, Work Hard. Be Nice.: How Two Inspired Teachers Created the Most Promising Schools in America 36, 135, 187 (2009).

CHAPTER 2: THE INFINITE POWER OF GRAMMAR

(1) **The Syntax of Sentencing:** b. "Look, Ms. Hester, the crime you committed warrants a significant punishment—but I think you are genuinely sorry for the harm you have caused, and I think you are also really committed to being a productive member of society."

(2) **The Syntax of Sports:** For more on Buddy Ryan, see "Buddy Ryan, Defensive Architect of 1985 Bears, Dies at 85," *Chicago Tribune*, June 28, 2016.

(3) **The Syntax of Retail:**

Fitch & Abercrombie	→	Abercrombie & Fitch
Gamble & Proctor	→	Proctor & Gamble
Deluca & Dean	→	Dean & Deluca
Decker & Black	→	Black & Decker
Poor's & Standard	→	Standard & Poor, as in "S&P 500"
Gabbana & Dolce	→	Dolce & Gabbana
Wesson & Smith	→	Smith & Wesson

- The name of the pharmaceutical company is "Johnson & Johnson." The name of the candy is "M&M's."

(4) **Child Custody:** "Other than Mr. Macondo's unsubstantiated claims, there is no evidence that Ms. Macondo will flee with José to Colombia, a country she was desperate to leave."

(5) **The Syntax of Style:** Ambrose Burnside $\rightarrow$ Sideburns

CHAPTER 3: THE RULE OF THREE

(1) **Children:**
   - C. S. Lewis: *The Lion, the Witch, and the <u>Wardrobe</u>*
     —C. S. Lewis, THE LION, THE WITCH, AND THE WARDROBE: THE CHRONICLES OF NARNIA BOOK 1 (1950)

   - *The Little Engine That Could*: "I think I can. I think I can. <u>I think I can</u>."
     —Watty Piper, THE LITTLE ENGINE THAT COULD (Penguin ed., 2005)

   - *Superman*: "It's a bird. It's a <u>plane</u>. It's Superman!"
     —THE ADVENTURES OF SUPERMAN (ABC television broadcast, 1952), *available at* https://www.youtube.com/watch?v=Q2l4bz1FT8U. The phrase "It's a bird, it's a plane, it's Superman!" appeared as dialogue in the introduction to every episode of the series.

   - The Big Bad Wolf: "I'll huff, and I'll puff, and <u>I'll blow your house down</u>."
     —Jacob Josephs, ENGLISH FAIRY TALES (1890)

(2) **Slogans:**
   - "Defending. Empowering. Influencing."
     Answer: American Civil Liberties Union (ACLU). ACLU, https://www.aclu.org

- "We build strength, stability, and self-reliance through shelter."
  Answer: Habitat for Humanity. *Annual Report FY 2016*, HABITAT FOR HUMANITY, https://www.habitat.org/sites/default/files/annual-report-2016.pdf
- "Helping youth is a key to building a more conscientious, responsible, and productive society."
  Answer: Boy Scouts of America. *About the Boy Scouts of America*, BOY SCOUTS OF AMERICA, http://www.scouting.org/about.aspx

(3) **Alliteration:**

"It is not from the benevolence of the butcher, the brewer, or the <u>baker</u> that we expect our dinner, but from their regard to their own interest."

—Adam Smith, The Wealth of Nations (1776)

"In subsequent cases also, we have recognized the fundamental right of parents to make decisions concerning the <u>care</u>, custody, and control of their children."

—Justice Sandra Day O'Connor, Troxel v. Granville (2000)

"We are a free clinic staffed by Michigan Law students that provides Unemployment Insurance advocacy, <u>advice</u>, and assistance to Michigan workers."

—website of Unemployment Insurance Clinic
at the University of Michigan Law School

(4) **Titles:**

- Sheryl Sandberg, *Lean In: Women, Work, and the Will to Lead*
- Richard H. Thaler and Cass R. Sunstein, *Nudge: Improving Decisions About Health, Wealth, and Happiness*

- Steven Levitt and Stephen Dubner, *Superfreakonomics: Global Cooling, Patriotic Prostitutes, and Why Suicide Bombers Should Buy Life Insurance*
- Doris Kearns Goodwin, *The Bully Pulpit: Theodore Roosevelt, William Howard Taft, and the Golden Age of Journalism*

(5) **Ugly Side:**

- "Segregation now. Segregation tomorrow. Segregation forever!"

  —former governor of Alabama George Wallace, inauguration address, January 14, 1963
- "Gas, Grass, or Ass. Nobody rides for free."

  —bumper sticker targeted by anti-human-trafficking groups
- "Remember the weak, meek, and ignorant are always good targets."

  —memo given to unscrupulous bond sellers in Tom Furlong, *The Keating Indictment: Targets of Bond Sellers: The "Weak, Meek, Ignorant,"* L.A. TIMES, Sept. 19, 1990
- "We can delay and effectively stop for a temporary period of indefinite length the number of immigrants into the United States. We could do this by simply advising our consuls to put every obstacle in the way and to require additional evidence and to resort to various administrative devices which would postpone and postpone and postpone the granting of the visas."

  —memo by Breckinridge Long to state department officials about how to avoid offering visas to Jewish refugees, June 26, 1940
- "Ein Volk, Ein Reich, Ein Führer." (Translation: "One People, One Nation, One Leader.")

  —slogan of Adolf Hitler and the Nazi Party

CHAPTER 4: SOUND AND SENSE

(1) **Film:** (A) Alma Reville (Hitchcock's wife). When accepting the American Film Institute's Lifetime Achievement Award in 1979, here is how Hitchcock honored the many roles Alma played in his life: "I beg to mention by name only four people who have given me the most affection, appreciation, encouragement, and constant collaboration. The first of the four is a film editor, the second is a scriptwriter, the third is the mother of my daughter, Pat, and the fourth is as fine a cook as ever performed miracles in a domestic kitchen. And their names are Alma Reville." American Film Institute, *Alfred Hitchcock Accepts the AFI Life Achievement Award in 1979*, YOUTUBE (Apr. 16, 2009), https://www.youtube.com/watch?v=pb5VdGCQFOM.

(2) **Supreme Court:** (E) Justice Elena Kagan. She, along with Justice Samuel Alito and Justice Sonia Sotomayor, went to college at Princeton.

(3) **Novels:**

Final Version	Earlier Draft
To Kill a Mockingbird	"Atticus"
The Lord of the Rings	"The War of the Ring"
Catch-22	"Catch-11"
Pride and Prejudice	"First Impressions"
Dracula	"The Dead Un-Dead"
War and Peace	"All's Well That Ends Well"
1984	"The Last Man in Europe"
The Sound and the Fury	"Twilight"
The Grapes of Wrath	"The Great Pig Sticking"
The Lord of the Flies	"Strangers From Within"
The Great Gatsby	"Trimalchio in West Egg"

(4) **Stand-Up Comedy:** Chris Rock

(5) **Pixar:** For an in-depth discussion of the "Braintrust" and other creative practices used by Pixar, check out Ed Catmull & Amy Wallace, CREATIVITY, INC.: OVERCOMING THE UNSEEN FORCES THAT STAND IN THE WAY OF TRUE INSPIRATION (New York: Random House, 2014).

CHAPTER 5: THE POWER OF THE PARTICULAR

(1) **Rolls-Royce:** For more on David Ogilvy's approach to advertising, check out David Ogilvy, CONFESSIONS OF AN ADVERTISING MAN (New York: Atheneum, 1963).

(2) **A Day in the Life:**

Single-Day Story	Authors/Directors
Ulysses (1922)	James Joyce
Die Hard (1988)	John McTiernan
Mrs. Dalloway (1925)	Virginia Woolf
Rebel Without a Cause (1955)	Nicholas Ray
High Noon (1952)	Fred Zinnemann
Ferris Bueller's Day Off (1986)	John Hughes
Saturday (2005)	Ian McEwan
Do Androids Dream of Electric Sheep? (1968)	Philip K. Dick
Cosmopolis (2003)	Don DeLillo
Seize the Day (1956)	Saul Bellow
After Dark (2004)	Haruki Murakami

(3) **Unparticular:** For the whole essay, check out *How to Write About Africa*, 92 GRANTA: THE MAGAZINE OF NEW WRITING, Jan. 19, 2006, *available at* https://granta.com/how-to-write-about-africa/.

(4) **State of the Union:** The president who started the tradition of inviting an ordinary citizen was Ronald Reagan.

(5) **Caddy Compson:** (D) *The Sound and the Fury.*

CHAPTER 6: USELESSLY ACCURATE

(1) **Design:** (D) Apple.

(2) **Conspicuous Composition:** (D) Thorstein Veblen.

(3) **Time Saver:** For the full essay, check out *On Writing Well*, FOR-EIGN POLICY, Feb. 15, 2013, *available at* http://foreignpolicy.com/ww2013/02/15/on-writing-well/.

(4) **Syllable Saver:** (E) Robert Creeley.

(5) **Clutter:**

Passage 1:

Every word that serves no <u>function</u>, every long word that could be a short word, every adverb that carries the same meaning that is already in the verb, every passive construction that leaves the reader <u>unsure</u> of who is doing what: these are the thousand and one adulterants that <u>weaken</u> the strength of a sentence. And they usually occur, ironically, in proportion to <u>education</u> and rank.

Passage 2 (added words are in **bold**):

Far too many Americans are prevented from doing useful work because they never **really** learned to fully express themselves. Contrary to **what is the** general belief, writing isn't something that only "writers" do; writing is a basic skill for getting through life. Yet most American adults are **absolutely** terrified of the prospect—ask a middle-aged engineer to write **up** a report and you'll see something close to panic. Writing, however, isn't a special language that belongs only to English teachers and a few other sensitive **and educated** souls who have a "gift for words." Writing is thinking on paper. Anyone who thinks clearly should be able to write clearly—about any subject **in the world** at all.

CHAPTER 7: CORRESPONDING IDEAS
IN CORRESPONDING FORMS: QUESTIONS

(1) **Politics:**

"Better to be despised for too anxious apprehensions than <u>ruined</u> by too confident a security."
—Edmund Burke, *Reflections on the French Revolution* (1790)

"When all think alike, <u>no one</u> thinks very much."
—Walter Lippman, *The Stakes of Diplomacy* (1915)

"I like the dreams of the <u>future</u> more than the history of the past. So good night. I will dream on, always fancying that Mrs. Adams and yourself are by my side marking the progress and the obliquities of ages and countries."
—Thomas Jefferson, letter to John Adams (1816)

(2) **Poetry:**

Letters: l a n e o
"Laugh, and the world laughs with you / Weep, and you weep <u>alone</u>."
—Ella Wheeler Wilcox, "Solitude" (1883)

Letters: c e f n e s
"Good <u>fences</u> make good neighbors."
—Robert Frost, "Mending Wall" (1914)

Letters: u r p l e y

"I love thee freely, as men strive for right. / I love thee <u>purely</u>, as they turn from praise."

—Elizabeth Barrett Browning, "How Do I Love Thee?" (1850)

(3) **Marketing:**

"Expect more. Pay less." → Target

"Carbs to compete. Electrolytes to replenish." → Gatorade

"American by birth. Rebel by choice." → Harley Davidson

"Live in your world. Play in ours." → PlayStation

"Your vision. Our future." → Olympus Cameras

(4) **Movies:**

"She brought a <u>small</u> town to its feet and a huge corporation to its <u>knees</u>."

—*Erin Brockovich* (2000)

"Just because they serve you doesn't mean they <u>like</u> you."

—*Clerks* (1994)

"The true story of a <u>real</u> fake."

—*Catch Me If You Can* (2002)

"The thing that won't die, in the nightmare that won't <u>end</u>."

—*The Terminator* (1984)

"The world's most dangerous times created the world's most dangerous <u>group</u>."

—*Straight Outta Compton* (2015)

"Fear can <u>hold</u> you prisoner. <u>Hope</u> can set you free."

—*Shawshank Redemption* (1994)

"Blood lost. <u>Life</u> found."

—*The Revenant* (2015)

"At the <u>end</u> of the universe lies the beginning of vengeance."

—*Star Trek 2: The Wrath of Khan* (1982)

(5) **Authors:** Identify the author.
"It was the best of times, it was the worst of times."
(A) Charles Murray
(B) Charles Baxter
(C) Charles Dickens
(D) Ray Charles

"How vain it is to sit down to write when you have not stood up to live."
(A) Henry Wadsworth Longfellow
(B) Henry David Thoreau
(C) Patrick Henry
(D) Thierry Henry

"The peculiar circumstances of the moment may render a measure more or less wise, but cannot render it more or less constitutional."
(A) Justice Thurgood Marshall
(B) Justice John Marshall
(C) Justice John Marshall Harlan
(D) Justice John Roberts

<u>Note:</u> Justice John Marshall wrote the line in 1819 in an essay called "A Friend of the Constitution" for the *Alexandria Gazette*

in Virginia. Justice Roberts quoted it in his opinion in *National Federation of Independent Business v. Sebelius*, the 2012 case that upheld the individual mandate provision of the Affordable Care Act as constitutional.

CHAPTER 8: CLARITY AND COHERENCE

(1) **Food:** Lunchables.

(2) **Anadiplosis:**

- "Having power makes [totalitarian leadership] isolated; isolation breeds insecurity; insecurity breeds suspicion and fear; suspicion and fear breed violence."

  —Zbigniew Brzezinski, *The Permanent Purge: Politics in Soviet Totalitarianism* (1956)

- "Meaning requires content, content requires time, time requires resistance."

  —Karl Ove Knaussgaard, *My Struggle: Book I*, translated by Don Bartlett (2012)

- "If you didn't grow up like I did then you don't know, and if you don't know then it is probably better you don't judge."

  —Junot Díaz, *The Brief Wondrous Life of Oscar Wao* (2007)

- "Once you change your philosophy, you change your thought pattern. Once you change your thought pattern, you change your attitude. Once you change your attitude, it changes your behavior pattern and then you go on into some action. As long as you gotta sit-down philosophy, you'll have a sit-down thought pattern, and as long as you think that old sit-down thought, you'll be in some kind of sit-down action."

  —Malcolm X, "The Ballot or the Bullet" (1964)

- "There are certain social principles in human nature from which we may draw the most solid conclusions with respect to the conduct of individuals and communities. We love our families more than our neighbors; we love our neighbors more than our countrymen in general."

  —Alexander Hamilton, "Constitutional Convention of New York" (1788)

(3) **Kids:**

"Right now, honey, the world just wants us to <u>fit</u> in, and to <u>fit</u> in we just gotta be like everybody else."

—*The Incredibles* (2004)

"If you don't eat, you'll be <u>weak</u>. If you are <u>weak</u>, you'll be slow; if you are slow, you'll die."

—*Kubo and the Two Strings* (2016)

"That buzzing noise means something. Now, the only reason for making a buzzing noise that I know of is because you are . . . a bee! And the only reason for being a bee is to make <u>honey</u>. And the only reason for making <u>honey</u> is so I can eat it."

—A. A. Milne, *Winnie the Pooh and the <u>Honey</u> Tree* (1966)

(4) **Law:**

All of us recognize this principle when a good <u>lawyer</u> tries to teach us something new. That <u>lawyer</u> will always try to connect some <u>case</u> we already <u>decided</u> to whatever new <u>case</u> we are trying to <u>resolve</u>.

(5) **Movies:**

"They call for you: The general who became a slave; the slave who became a gladiator; the gladiator who defied an emperor. Striking story."

(A) *The Patriot*

(B) *Braveheart*

(C) *The Rock*

(D) *Gladiator*

"Fear is the path to the dark side. Fear leads to anger. Anger leads to hate. Hate leads to suffering."

(A) *Star Wars: The Phantom Menace*

(B) *Star Wars: The Force Awakens*

(C) *Poltergeist*

(D) *Poltergeist II: The Other Side*

"If we don't get this, we don't get the shot. If we don't get the shot, we don't get the movie. If we don't get the movie, we're all up the creek."

(A) George Lucas to Steven Spielberg on the set of *Raiders of the Lost Ark*

(B) Steven Spielberg to George Lucas on the set of *Raiders of the Lost Ark*

(C) George Lucas to Steven Spielberg on the set of *Jurassic Park*

(D) Steven Spielberg to George Lucas on the set of *Jurassic Park*

[Note: You can see the Lucas-Spielberg interaction in the HBO Documentary *Spielberg* (2017).]

CHAPTER 9: GOOD SENTENCES

(1) **Founding Father:** (B) Benjamin Franklin

(2) **Founding Mother:** (C) Abigail Adams

(3) **Cartoons:** (D) never

(4) **Retail:** (D) Walmart

(5) **Soccer:** Mia Hamm

NOTES

CHAPTER 1

1 **"descriptions of things"** Tim Adams, The Undoing Project *Review*: "Psychology's Lennon and McCartney", THE GUARDIAN (Dec. 11, 2016).

2 **"framing"** *See, e.g.*, Amos Tversky & Daniel Kahneman, *Prospect Theory: An Analysis of Decision Under Risk*, 47.2 ECONOMETRICA 263–292 (1979); Amos Tversky & Daniel Kahneman, *The Framing of Decisions and the Psychology of Choice*, 211.4481 SCIENCE 453–458 (1981); Amos Tversky & Daniel Kahneman, *Rational Choice and the Framing of Decisions*, 59.4 JOURNAL OF BUSINESS S251–S278 (1986).

2 **"survival rate"** Amos Tversky & Daniel Kahneman, *Rational Choice and the Framing of Decisions*, 59.4 JOURNAL OF BUSINESS S254 (1986).

2 **"lean"** *See* Irwin P. Levin & Gary J. Gaeth, *How Consumers Are Affected by the Framing of Attribute Information Before and After Consuming the Product*, 15.3 JOURNAL OF CONSUMER RESEARCH 374–378 (1988).

2 **"Elizabeth Loftus"** *See, e.g.*, Elizabeth F. Loftus & Guido Zanni, *Eyewitness Testimony: The Influence of the Wording of a Question*, 5.1 BULLETIN OF THE PSYCHONOMIC SOCIETY 86–88 (1975); Elizabeth F. Loftus, *Leading Questions and the Eyewitness Report*, 7.4 COGNITIVE PSYCHOLOGY 550–572 (1975).

2 **"broken headlight"** Elizabeth F. Loftus, *Leading Questions and the Eyewitness Report*, 7.4 COGNITIVE PSYCHOLOGY 562 (1975).

3 **"the words under the words"** Naomi Shihab Nye, *Words Under the Words*, *in* WORDS UNDER THE WORDS: SELECTED POEMS 36 (Portland: Far Corner Books, 1995).

5   **"case law in Michigan"** *Razmus v. Kirkhof Transformer*, 137 Mich. App. 311 (1984).

9   **"right sort of practice"** Anders Ericsson & Robert Pool, PEAK: SECRETS FROM THE NEW SCIENCE OF EXPERTISE xxi (Boston: Houghton Mifflin Harcourt, 2016).

9   **"effective training techniques"** *Id.* at 99.

9   **"full attention"** *Id.*

9   **"current abilities"** *Id.*

10   **"feeling goes away"** This quote is often attributed to Robert Maynard Hutchins, president of the University of Chicago from 1929 to 1945. It seems to come from an interview in a 1938 magazine profile, but the structure of the sentence does not make it clear whether the author has paraphrased Hutchins or someone Hutchins referenced during the interview. *See* J. P. McEvoy, *Garlands for the Living*, AMERICAN MERCURY, Dec. 1938, at 482–484 ("The secret of my abundant health is that whenever the impulse to exercise comes over me, I lie down until it passes away."); *see also* Ralph Keyes, THE QUOTE VERIFIER: WHO SAID WHAT, WHERE, AND WHEN 59 (New York: St. Martin's Griffin, 2007).

11   **"done consistently and correctly"** Daniel F. Chambliss, CHAMPIONS: THE MAKING OF OLYMPIC SWIMMERS 213–216 (New York: William Morrow, 1988); *see also* Angela Duckworth, GRIT: THE POWER OF PASSION AND PERSEVERANCE 35–53 (New York: Scribner, 2016).

11   **"how ordinary success is"** Daniel F. Chambliss, CHAMPIONS: THE MAKING OF OLYMPIC SWIMMERS 81 (New York: William Morrow, 1988).

11   **"as fast as a court reporter"** Anne Lamott, BIRD BY BIRD: SOME INSTRUCTIONS ON WRITING AND LIFE 21 (New York: Anchor, 1995).

12   **"wastebasket"** *Letter From Ernest Hemingway, Novelist, to F. Scott Fitzgerald* (May 28, 1934), *in* LETTERS OF NOTE: AN ECLECTIC COLLECTION OF CORRESPONDENCE DESERVING OF A WIDER AUDIENCE 229 (Shaun Usher ed., San Francisco: Chronicle, 2014).

12   **"with your nose"** The words of this quote can be easily found on the internet. But I have been unable to connect it to one of Oates's specific works. It is usually cited with only an attribution to her name. A possible origin comes from an oral interview Oates gave more than 30 years ago. *See* Helen Trinca, *Creatures of Habit Revealed in Mason Currey's Book*

"Daily Rituals," AUSTRALIAN, Nov. 2, 2013 ("Joyce Carol Oates is one of the most prolific modern writers but in 1987 told an interviewer that 'getting the first draft finished is like pushing a peanut with your nose across a very dirty floor.'").

15 **"custody dispute"** Eldar Shafir, Itamar Simonson & Amos Tversky, *Reason-Based Choice*, 49.1–2 COGNITION 11–36 (1993).

19 **"gender discrimination"** Jeffrey Toobin, *Heavyweight*, NEW YORKER (Mar. 11, 2013), *available at* http://www.newyorker.com/magazine/2013/03/11/heavyweight-ruth-bader-ginsburg ("Henceforth, she changed her claim to 'gender discrimination.'").

24 **"open debate"** William Domnarski, RICHARD POSNER 97–98 (Oxford: Oxford University Press, 2016).

24 **"hospital"** For discussions on a related question—"Should doctors call patients by their first names?"—see Robert D. Gillete, Andrew Filak & Charles Thorne, *First Name or Last Name: Which Do Patients Prefer?*, 5.5 JOURNAL OF THE AMERICAN BOARD OF FAMILY MEDICINE 517–522 (1992); Michael Lavin, *What Doctors Should Call Their Patients*, 14.3 JOURNAL OF MEDICAL ETHICS 129–131 (1988).

24 **"Professor"** *See* Eugene Volokh, *Should Law Students Call Professors 'Professor X' or Use First Names?*, WASHINGTON POST: VOLOKH CONSPIRACY (Aug. 22, 2016), *available at* https://www.washingtonpost.com/news/volokh-conspiracy/wp/2016/08/22/should-law-students-call-professors-professor-x-or-use-first-names/?utm_term=.6f0a8d755ea9; Stephanie Francis Ward, *Should Law Students Call Professors by Their First Names?*, ABA JOURNAL (Aug. 23, 2016), *available at* http://www.abajournal.com/news/article/should_students_call_law_professors_by_their_first_names.

CHAPTER 2

28 **"Why I Write"** Joan Didion, *Why I Write*, N.Y. TIMES (Dec. 5, 1976), *available at* https://www.nytimes.com/1976/12/05/archives/why-i-write-why-i-write.html. The title is taken from an essay of the same name written by George Orwell in 1946. George Orwell, *Why I Write*, 4 GANGREL (1946); *see also* George Orwell, THE COLLECTED ESSAYS, JOURNALISM AND LETTERS OF GEORGE ORWELL: AN AGE LIKE THIS, 1920–1940 1–7 (Sonia Orwell & Ian Angus eds., New York: Harcourt Brace, 1968).

30 **"Confrontation Clause"** U.S. Const. amend. VI ("In all criminal prosecutions, the accused shall enjoy the right to . . . be confronted with the witnesses against him . . . .").

30 **"Federal Appellate Clinic"** Students in Michigan's Federal Appellate Clinic litigate cases in the Sixth Circuit Court of Appeals pro bono on behalf of clients who are too poor to hire quality appellate lawyers of their own.

30 **"fornicating under a little-used statute"** Richard C. Wydick, *Plain English for Lawyers*, 66.4 California Law Review 727, 747 (1978), *available at* http://scholarship.law.berkeley.edu/cgi/viewcontent.cgi?article=2362&context=californialawreview.

31 **"Stephen King"** Stephen King, On Writing: A Memoir of the Craft 151 (New York: Scribner, 2000); *see also, e.g.*, Frank Budgen, James Joyce and the Making of Ulysses 9–22 (Oxford: Oxford University Press, 1934), reprinted in James Joyce: Interviews & Recollections 77 (E. H. Mikhail ed., London: Macmillan, 1990), *cited in* Hugh Kenner, Ulysses 5 n.12 1987).

40 **"website to help writers"** UVA Writing Program Instructor Site, http://faculty.virginia.edu/schoolhouse/WP/WP.html (last visited Dec. 1, 2017).

42 **"harder to unpack them"** *Id.*

43 **"sentences that move"** *Letter from F. Scott Fitzgerald to Frances Scott Fitzgerald* (Spring 1938), *in* F. Scott Fitzgerald: A Life in Letters (Matthew Bruccoli ed., New York: Scribner, 2015).

46 **"active constructions aren't always the best choice"** Steven Pinker, *Passive Resistance*, Atlantic (Nov. 2014), *available at* https://www.theatlantic.com/magazine/archive/2014/11/passive-resistance/380787/.

47 **"American Heritage Dictionary"** Past members of this panel have included Junot Díaz, Isaac Asimov, Barbara Kingsolver, Joan Didion, Amy Tan, Henry Louis Gates, Anne Curzan, David Foster Wallace, William F. Buckley, Rita Dove, Garrison Keillor, Leslie Marmon Silko, and Supreme Court Justice Antonin Scalia. It's a pretty distinguished group.

47 **"implicating him in the charged offense"** Brief for Petitioner at 23–24, *Crawford v. Washington*, 541 U.S. 36 (2003) (No. 02-9410).

48 **"No shots were fired, no money was taken, and no one was injured"** Brief for Respondent O'Brien at 2, *United States v. O'Brien*, 560 U.S. 218 (2010) (No. 08-1569).

48 **"Kennedy wrote"** *United States v. O'Brien,* 560 U.S. 218, 222 (2010).

49 **"Blank was blanked by blank"** June Casagrande, *A Word, Please: Taking a Deeper Look at the Passive Voice*, L.A. TIMES (Oct. 17, 2014), *available at* http://www.latimes.com/tn-gnp-a-word-please-taking-a-deeper-look-at -the-passive-voice-20141017-story.html.

49 **"Nature journals prefer authors to"** *Writing for a Nature Journal*, NATURE, *available at* https://www.nature.com/authors/author_resources/how _write.html.

49 **"Use active voice when suitable"** *Writing Tips: Active Voice and Passive Voice*, BIOMEDICAL EDITOR, *available at* https://www.biomedicaleditor. com/active-voice.html.

CHAPTER 3

51 **"Clint Eastwood movie"** THE GOOD, THE BAD, AND THE UGLY (Produzioni Europee Associate 1966).

52 **"I was simmering"** In conversation with fellow writer John Townsend Trowbridge. *See* John Townsend Trowbridge, *Reminiscences of Walt Whitman*, ATLANTIC MONTHLY (Feb. 1902), *available at* https://www .theatlantic.com/past/docs/unbound/poetry/whitman/walt.htm.

52 **"Location. Location. Location."** For the disputed origins of this mantra, see William Safire, *Location, Location, Location*, N.Y. TIMES MAGAZINE (June 26, 2009), *available at* http://www.nytimes.com/2009/06/28/ magazine/28FOB-onlanguage-t.html.

52 **"We obsess over every ingredient"** *Chipotle*, CULTIVATOR, *available at* http://www.cultivatorads.com/work/chipotle/.

53 **"Practice. Practice. Practice."** Michael Pollack, *The Origins of That Famous Carnegie Hall Joke*, N.Y. TIMES (Nov. 27, 2009), *available at* http:// www.nytimes.com/2009/11/29/nyregion/29fyi.html.

53 **"Marcia! Marcia! Marcia!"** *Her Sister's Shadow*, THE BRADY BUNCH (ABC television broadcast Nov. 19, 1971), *available at* https://www.youtube .com/watch?v=-yZHveWFvqM.

53 **"unexpected brain hemorrhage"** Lord Alfred Tennyson, "Break, Break, Break" (1842). Hallam was also the subject of Tennyson's longer and more famous poem "In Memoriam A. H. H." (1849).

53 **"the first and the last stanza"** Lord Alfred Tennyson, "Break, Break, Break" (1842).

> *Break, break, break,*
> > *On thy cold gray stones, O Sea!*
> *And I would that my tongue could utter*
> > *The thoughts that arise in me*
>
> . . . .
>
> *Break, break, break*
> > *At the foot of thy crags, O Sea!*
> *But the tender grace of a day that is dead*
> > *Will never come back to me.* (emphasis added)

53 **"Dance, Dance, Dance"** Haruki Murakami, DANCE, DANCE, DANCE (New York: Vintage Books, 1995).

54 **"Agua, Agua, Agua"** Pat Mora, AGUA, AGUA, AGUA (Culver City, CA: Good Year Books, 1996).

54 **"helpfully multilingual"** The "I divorce you. I divorce you. I divorce you" example is evidence of this as well.

54 **"Don't, don't, don't"** John Cheever, *The Five-Forty-Eight*, NEW YORKER (Apr. 10, 1954), *available at* http://www.newyorker.com/magazine/1954/04/10/the-five-forty-eight.

54 **"be a good sport"** Emma Cline, *Northeast Regional*, NEW YORKER (Apr. 10, 2017), *available at* http://www.newyorker.com/magazine/2017/04/10/northeast-regional.

54 **"No fees. No expiration. No kidding."** *Promotional Gift Card $30*, TARGET, *available at* https://bit.ly/2WrFSsQ.

55 **"Change lives. Change organizations. Change the world."** STANFORD GRADUATE SCHOOL OF BUSINESS, *available at* https://www.gsb.stanford.edu/.

55 **"Wings. Beer. Sports."** Buffalo Wild Wings (@BWWings), TWITTER, *available at* http://twitter.com/bwwings.

55 **"For free. For everyone. Forever."** KHAN ACADEMY, https://www.khanacademy.org.

55 **"New Year. New Adventure. New Sale."** Southwest Airlines (@SouthwestAir), TWITTER, *available at* https://twitter.com/SouthwestAir.

55 **"The Few. The Proud. The Marines."** Jeff Schogol, *Marines Are Once Again "The Few, The Proud,"* MARINE CORPS TIMES (Mar. 30, 2017), *available at* https://www.marinecorpstimes.com/articles/iconic-marine-recruiting-slogan-returns.

55 **"first draft of the Declaration"** *Jefferson's "Original Rough Draught" of the Declaration of Independence*, THE PAPERS OF THOMAS JEFFERSON, VOLUME 1: 1760–1776, at 423–428 (Princeton: Princeton University Press, 1950), *available at* https://jeffersonpapers.princeton.edu/selected-documents/jefferson%E2%80%99s-%22original-rough-draught%22-declaration-independence-0.

55 **"'mutilations' and 'depredations'"** Letter from Thomas Jefferson to Robert Walsh (1818), *reprinted in* 1 Henry Stephens Randall, THE LIFE OF THOMAS JEFFERSON 178 n.2 (Philadelphia: J. B. Lippincott, 1858).

56 **"life, liberty, and the pursuit of happiness"** *See, e.g.,* Scott D. Gerber, TO SECURE THESE RIGHTS: THE DECLARATION OF INDEPENDENCE AND CONSTITUTIONAL INTERPRETATION 28 (New York: New York University Press, 1996); Kenneth D. Stern, *John Locke and the Declaration of Independence*, 15 CLEVELAND-MARSHALL LAW REVIEW 186 (1966), *available at* https://engagedscholarship.csuohio.edu/cgi/viewcontent.cgi?referer=https://www.google.com/&httpsredir=1&article=3019&context=clevstlrev.

56 **"the ear welcomes the relief"** Ward Farnsworth, FARNSWORTH'S CLASSICAL ENGLISH RHETORIC 71 (Boston: David R. Godine, 2010).

57 **"the greatest judicial opinion of the last hundred years"** Richard Posner, LAW AND LITERATURE 346 (3d ed., Cambridge: Harvard University Press, 2009).

57 **"Mr. Herbert Spencer's Social Statics"** *Lochner v. New York*, 198 U.S. 45, 75 (1905) (Holmes, J., dissenting) (emphasis added).

58 **"It was the opposite of my life at school"** William Finnegan, BARBARIAN DAYS: A SURFING LIFE 8 (New York: Penguin Books, 2015).

58 **"That's our goal"** For another example of the Rule of Three in Reverse, check out this sentence in *The Writing Life* by Annie Dillard: "The page is jealous and tyrannical; the page is made out of time and matter; the page always wins." Annie Dillard, THE WRITING LIFE 57 (New York: Harper Perennial, 2013).

59 **"visible speech"** John DeFrancis, VISIBLE SPEECH: THE DIVERSE ONENESS OF WRITING SYSTEMS 248–253 (Honolulu: University of Hawaii Press, 1989). DeFrancis drew his title from the phonetics system developed by Alexander Melville Bell, a 19th-century phonetician who posited the idea of a universal alphabet.

CHAPTER 4

78 **"give offense"** Alexander Pope, *An Essay on Criticism, in* SELECTED POETRY 1 (Oxford: Oxford University Press, 2008).

78 **"must seem an echo to the sense"** *Id.* at 10.

78 **"letter to a former student"** *Letter from Robert Frost to John Bartlett* (July 4, 1913), *in* THE LETTERS OF ROBERT FROST, VOLUME 1: 1886–1920 121–123 (Cambridge: Harvard University Press, 2014).

78 **"merge sound and sense together"** *Id.*

78 **"be it of prose or verse"** *Id.* at 123.

79 **"Of course I stole the title for this essay from George Orwell"** Joan Didion, *Why I Write*, N.Y. TIMES (Dec. 5, 1976).

79 **"the sound they share"** *Id.*

79 **"listen to me"** *Id.* (emphasis in original).

79 **"Grammar is a piano I play by ear"** *Id.*

79 **"rhythms of words and sentences and paragraphs"** Joan Didion, THE YEAR OF MAGICAL THINKING 7 (New York: Vintage Books, 2007).

80 **"how improvement happens"** Atul Gawande, *Personal Best*, NEW YORKER (Oct. 3, 2011), *available at* http://www.newyorker.com/magazine/2011/10/03/personal-best.

80 **"interferes with your accuracy of listening"** *Id.*

81 **"Her ear provides external judgment"** *Id.*

81 **"outside ears."** *Id.*

81 **"What we hear as we are singing is not what the audience hears"** *Id.*

81 **"on their own, sentences are implacably honest"** Verlyn Klinkenborg, *The Trouble with Intentions*, N.Y. TIMES: OPINIONATOR (Sept. 24, 2010), *available at* https://opinionator.blogs.nytimes.com/2012/09/24/the-trouble-with-intentions/?_r=0.

81 **"They are what they are and they say what they say"** *Id.*

81 **"obvious flaws the reader now has to suffer through"** *Id.* ("Why didn't the writers catch these mistakes?").

81 **"The sentence, as written, was invisible to them"** *Id.*

81 **"address this problem"** Verlyn Klinkenborg, SEVERAL SHORT SENTENCES ABOUT WRITING 50 (New York: Knopf, 2012).

83 **"(1) what is this case about? (2) why should I win?"** Chief Justice John G. Roberts Jr., *Interviews With United States Supreme Court Justices*, SCRIBES JOURNAL OF LEGAL WRITING 5, 25 (Bryan Garner ed., 2010).

85 **"But you pretty much always catch it when you're reading out loud"** Kristin Hohenadel, *Say It Out Loud: How David Sedaris Makes His Writing Better*, FAST COMPANY (Apr. 15, 2013), *available at* https://www.fastcompany.com/1682768/say-it-out-loud-how-david-sedaris-makes-his-writing-better.

85 **"Except for you"** Charles Champlin, *Alma Reville Hitchcock—the Unsung Partner*, L.A. TIMES (Jul. 29, 1982), *available at* https://the.hitchcock.zone/wiki/Los_Angeles_Times_(29/Jul/1982)_-_Alma_Reville_Hitchcock,_The_Unsung_Partner.

86 **"telling me what I could do better"** Interview by Bryan Garner with Justice Elena Kagan, *in Full Transcript of Bryan A. Garner's Interview with Elena Kagan*, ABA JOURNAL, (Sept. 2012), *available at* https://bit.ly/2VbZRip.

88 **"He started riding around and going to clubs with me"** Amy Schumer, THE GIRL WITH THE LOWER BACK TATTOO 166 (New York: Gallery Books, 2016).

89 **"Giving the Braintrust no power"** Ed Catmull & Amy Wallace, CREATIVITY, INC.: OVERCOMING THE UNSEEN FORCES THAT STAND IN THE WAY OF TRUE INSPIRATION 92–93 (New York: Random House, 2014).

89 **"they should be at the table"** *Id.* at 105.

CHAPTER 5

100 **"put the listener in the burning house"** Sonia Sotomayor, MY BELOVED WORLD 211 (New York: Knopf, 2013).

100 **"put them in the shoes of the accused or victim"** *Id.*

100 **"make a story real."** *Id.*

100 **"argues for its truth"** Mary Karr, THE ART OF MEMOIR 72 (New York: Harper, 2016); *see also* Mary Karr, *Sacred Carnality*, NEW YORKER (Oct. 11, 2015), *available at* http://www.newyorker.com/books/page-turner/sacred-carnality.

101 **"Ph.D. in developmental psychology"** Brief for Petitioners at 7, *Adoptive Couple v. Baby Girl*, 133 S. Ct. 2552 (2013) (No. 12-229), *available at* http://sblog.s3.amazonaws.com/wp-content/uploads/2013/02/12-399-pet-brief.pdf.

101 **"undergone seven unsuccessful attempts at in vitro fertilization"** *Id.*

101 **"delivery room"** *Id.* at 9.

101 **"cut the umbilical cord"** *Id.* Blatt's brief, of course, takes a certain, pro-adoptive-couple approach to the case. For a more complete overview, I recommend (1) reading all the briefs in the case, (2) listening to Radiolab's "Adoptive Couple vs. Baby Girl" episode, or (3), best of all, doing both.

106 **"facts . . . I can picture"** THE BEST AMERICAN SHORT STORIES 1985 xvi (John Updike & Shannon Reverel eds., Boston: Houghton Mifflin Harcourt, 1985); *see also* John Updike, MORE MATTER: ESSAYS AND CRITICISM 182 (New York: Random House, 1999).

107 **"the electric clock"** *Our History*, OGILVY, *available at* http://www.ogilvy .com/our-history/.

108 **"poverty in the South Bronx"** Adrian Nicole LeBlanc, RANDOM FAMILY: LOVE, DRUGS, TROUBLE, AND COMING OF AGE IN THE BRONX (New York: Scribner, 2004).

108 **"homeless children"** Andrea Elliott, *Invisible Child*, N.Y. TIMES (Dec. 9, 2013), *available at* http://www.nytimes.com/projects/2013/invisible -child/#/?chapt=1.

108 **"impoverished settlement in India"** Katherine Boo, BEHIND THE BEAUTIFUL FOREVERS: LIFE, DEATH, AND HOPE IN A MUMBAI UNDERCITY (New York: Random House, 2012).

109 **"How to Write About Africa"** Binyavanga Wainaina, *How to Write About Africa*, 92 GRANTA: THE MAGAZINE OF NEW WRITING (Jan. 19, 2006), *available at* https://granta.com/how-to-write-about-africa/.

110 **"Lenny Skutnik"** Ronald Reagan, *Address Before a Joint Session of the Congress Reporting on the State of the Union*, THE AMERICAN PRESIDENCY PROJECT (Jan. 26, 1982), *available at* http://www.presidency.ucsb.edu/documents/ address-before-joint-session-the-congress-reporting-the-state-the- union-2; *see also* Ronald Reagan, *Address Before a Joint Session of the Congress Reporting on the State of the Union*, THE REAGAN LIBRARY (Jan. 26, 1982), *available at* https://www.reaganlibrary.gov/research/speeches/20685e.

Multiple sources cite Reagan's speech as the first time a president called out an ordinary citizen for recognition during the State of the Union. *See, e.g.*, Francis X. Clines, *Bonding as New Political Theater: Bring On the Babies and Cue the Yellow Dog*, N.Y. TIMES (Aug. 24, 1996), *available at* http://www.nytimes.com/1996/08/24/us/bonding-as-new-political -theater-bring-on-the-babies-and-cue-the-yellow-dog.html (referring to the feel-good trend Reagan started as "Skutnik Syndrome"); Merrill Fabray, *This Is Why U.S. Presidents Started Name-Dropping Their State of the Union Guests*, TIME (Jan. 12, 2016), *available at* http://time.com/4175037/skutnik-state-of-the-union-history/ (directly attributing the practice to Reagan); *Lenny Skutnik, CBO's Most Famous Employee, Retires*, CONGRESSIONAL BUDGET OFFICE (June 3, 2010), *available at* https://www.cbo.gov/publication/25080.

114   **"one significant detail"** This previously unpublished document was helpfully included by Noah A. Messing in Appendix A of his wonderful book THE ART OF ADVOCACY: BRIEFS, MOTIONS, AND WRITING STRATEGIES OF AMERICA'S BEST LAWYERS (New York: Wolters Kluwer, 2013).

CHAPTER 6

120   **"The story of how 7 Up got its name"** Andrew F. Smith, FOOD AND DRINK IN AMERICAN HISTORY: A "FULL COURSE" ENCYCLOPEDIA 808 (Santa Barbara: ABC-Clio, 2013) (cited in Jeffrey L. Rodengen, THE LEGEND OF DR PEPPER/7UP (Fort Lauderdale: Write Stuff Enterprises, 1995)).

120   **"Bib-Label Lithiated Lemon-Lime Soda"** *7UP*, DR PEPPER SNAPPLE GROUP, *available at* https://www.drpeppersnapplegroup.com/brands/7up.

121   **"tell everything"** 17 Voltaire, THE COMPLETE WORKS OF VOLTAIRE 520 (Oxford: The Voltaire Foundation, 1991) ("Le secret d'ennuyer est celui de tout dire.").

122   **"attention economies"** Richard Lanham, REVISING PROSE 21 (London: Pearson, 2007).

122   **"affront to efficiency"** Lanham makes this point nicely in *Revising Prose* when examining an overstuffed sentence written by an economist: "Why has there been no transfer here of economic thinking to economic prose," Lanham asks. "Why no transfer of power from argument to expression? Why do these writers, who study the efficient allocation of scarce resources, waste two thirds of their vital resource—the reader's attention?" Richard Lanham, REVISING PROSE 23 (2007).

124   **"maximally considerate writing"** David Foster Wallace, BOTH FLESH AND NOT: ESSAYS 261 (New York: Little, Brown, 2013).

126 **"saved humankind a net 230 hours of effort"** Stephen M. Walt, *On Writing Well*, FOREIGN POLICY (Feb. 15, 2013), *available at* http://foreignpolicy .com/2013/02/15/on-writing-well/.

127 **"We are a society strangling in unnecessary words"** William Zinsser, ON WRITING WELL: THE CLASSIC GUIDE TO WRITING NONFICTION 6 (New York: HarperCollins, 2016).

CHAPTER 7

137 **"We must fight!"** Thomas Kidd, PATRICK HENRY: FIRST AMONG PATRIOTS 97 (New York: Basics Books, 2011).

138 **"corresponding ideas expressed in corresponding forms"** Carl H. Klaus, A SELF MADE OF WORDS: CRAFTING A DISTINCTIVE PERSONA IN NONFICTION WRITING 62 (Iowa City: University of Iowa Press, 2014).

138 **"More saving. More doing."** THE HOME DEPOT, *available at* http://www .homedepot.com.

138 **"Keep the wisdom. Lose the lines."** Marilyn Kalfus & Colin Stewart, *Does Botox Look Its Age? It's 10 Years Old*, ORANGE COUNTY REGISTER (Apr. 15, 2012) *available at* https://bit.ly/2JLH5cA.

138 **"Fly like a CEO. Pay like a temp."** *Airline Slogans & Taglines*, BRANDING REFERENCE, *available at* https://brandingreference.com/ airline-slogans-taglines.

138 **"who's going to sit in the White House and who's going to be in the dog house"** Malcolm X, Speech at King Solomon Baptist Church, Detroit, Michigan (April 12, 1964).

139 **"symmetry is what we see at a glance"** Giora Hon & Bernard R. Goldstein, FROM SUMMETRIA TO SYMMETRY: THE MAKING OF A REVOLUTIONARY SCIENTIFIC CONCEPT 126 (New York: Springer, 2008).

141 **"readers and listeners strongly prefer coordinated elements of sentences to be parallel in structure"** *See* Lyn Frazier et al., *Parallel Structure: A Source of Facilitation in Sentence Comprehension*, 12.5 MEMORY & COGNITION 421 (1984), *available at* https://link.springer.com/content/pdf/10 .3758%2FBF03198303.pdf.

141 **"parallel structure effect"** *Id.*

141 **"the parallel version was more easily absorbed than the nonparallel version"** *Id.* at 426 ("The most striking aspect of these findings is the pervasiveness of the basic parallel structure effect.").

141   "that the preference for parallel structure . . . is not simply an aesthetic judgment" *Id.* at 422.

141   "we think it is wrong and ought to be restricted" *Letter from Abraham Lincoln to Alexander H. Stephens* (Dec. 22, 1860), *in* 6 THE COMPLETE WORKS OF ABRAHAM LINCOLN 85–86 (John G. & John Hay eds., New York: Tandy-Thomas, 1860), *available at* https://digital.lib.niu.edu/islandora/object/niu-lincoln%3A36652.

142   "Let no woman be kept from the ballot box because of her sex" Robin Van Auken & Louis Hunsinger Jr., WILLIAMSPORT: BOOMTOWN ON THE SUSQUEHANNA 57 (Charleston: Arcadia, 2004).

142   "unshakeable conviction" Stanley Fish, HOW TO WRITE A SENTENCE AND HOW TO READ ONE 48 (New York: HarperCollins, 2012).

142   "limit yourself to relatively small words" *Id.*

142   "they can be delivered in a click and a snap" *Id.* at 21.

142   "pithy pronouncement" *Id.* at 47.

142   "is another's lyric" *Cohen v. California*, 403 U.S. 15, 25 (1971).

143   "A page of history is worth a pound of logic" *New York Trust Co. v. Eisner*, 256 U.S. 345, 350 (1921).

CHAPTER 8

160   "fancy-sounding nonsense" Janny Scott, *Postmodern Gravity Deconstructed, Slyly*, N.Y. TIMES (May 18, 1996), *available at* http://www.nytimes.com/1996/05/18/nyregion/postmodern-gravity-deconstructed-slyly.html; *see also* Alan D. Sokal, *Transgressing the Boundaries: Towards a Transformative Hermeneutics of Quantum Gravity*, 46/47 SOCIAL TEXT 217 (1996), *available at* http://www.physics.nyu.edu/sokal/transgress_v2/transgress_v2_singlefile.html.

161   "Joseph Williams" Joseph Williams & Gregory Colomb, STYLE: TOWARD CLARITY AND GRACE 48 (Chicago: University of Chicago Press, 1990).

161   "as you begin a sentence" *Id.*

163   "the first five or six words of every sentence" *Id.* at 52.

164   "treated my parents with condescension" Richard Rodriguez, HUNGER OF MEMORY: THE EDUCATION OF RICHARD RODRIGUEZ 96 (New York: Dial Press, 2004).

CHAPTER 9

178 **"Spend more time reading"** Bryan A. Garner, Garner on Language and Writing 16 (Chicago: American Bar Association, 2009).

178 **"spend more time reading good prose"** *Id.*

178 **"the important thing is the way the writer uses the language"** Annie Dillard, The Writing Life 68 (New York: Harper Perennial, 2013).

179 **"much the way a mechanic might learn about an engine by taking it apart"** *Id.* at 36.

179 **"even Foxx's hair had muscles"** Bill James, The New Bill James Baseball Historical Abstract 891 (New York: Free Press, 2003).

179 **"buttermilk"** Ben Bradlee Jr., The Kid: The Immortal Life of Ted Williams 118 (New York: Little, Brown, 2013).

179 **"batting practice"** *Inning 6: The National Pastime*, Baseball (PBS television broadcast 1994).

179 **"the most gifted instrumentalist of all time"** *Jimi Hendrix Experience*, Rock & Roll Hall of Fame, *available at* https://www.rockhall.com/inductees/jimi-hendrix-experience.

180 **"Joseph Haydn"** Karl Geiringer, Haydn: A Creative Life in Music 21 (Berkeley: University of California Press, 1982) ("According to Johann Friedrich Rochlitz, Haydn once said: 'Proper teachers I have never had. I always started right away with the practical side, first in singing and in playing instruments, later in composition. I listened more than I studied, but I heard the finest music in all forms that was to be heard in my time, and of this there was much in Vienna. Oh, so much! I listened attentively and tried to turn to good account what most impressed me. Thus, little by little my knowledge and my ability were developed.").

180 **"Charlie Parker"** *See* Stanley Crouch, *An Apprenticeship in Blues and Swing, in* Kansas City Lightning: The Rise and Times of Charlie Parker 175 (New York: HarperCollins, 2013).

180 **"Aretha Franklin"** David Ritz, Respect: The Life of Aretha Franklin 72 (New York: Little, Brown, 2014) ("Aretha liked to hang out at our shop—not only because she was crazy, but because of the music. She also spent a lot of time in my room—I had a separate apartment-like setup in the mansion—where she'd sit in front of the hi-fi for hours on end. That's where she first heard Sarah Vaughan, Smokey's favorite. But she didn't stop with Sarah. She studied Ella Fitzgerald, Billie Holiday,

Carmen McRae, Anita O'Day, June Christy, Dakota Staton—anyone I had on the box. She got to a point where she could imitate these singers, lick for lick.").

180 **"spent hours imitating"** Roderick Conway Morris, *How Manet Was Influenced by the Artists of the Renaissance*, SPECTATOR (Aug. 3, 2013), *available at* https://www.spectator.co.uk/2013/08/how-manet-was-influenced-by-the-artists-of-the-renaissance/#.#.

181 **"writing is learned by imitation"** William Zinsser, WRITING TO LEARN viii (New York: Harper Perennial, 2013).

182 **"fell short in elegance of expression"** Benjamin Franklin & William Temple Franklin, 1 MEMOIRS OF THE LIFE AND WRITINGS OF BENJAMIN FRANKLIN 11 (London: H. Colburn, 1818).

184 **"Founding Mother"** Edith B. Gelles, ABIGAIL ADAMS: A WRITING LIFE (New York: Routledge, 2014).

184 **"Remember the Ladies"** *Abigail Adams to John Adams, 31 March 1776*, NATIONAL ARCHIVES: FOUNDERS ONLINE, *available at* http://founders.archives.gov/documents/Adams/04-01-02-0241.

185 **"Determined to educate myself on what a New Yorker cartoon was"** Bob Mankoff, *Chapter Four: Deconstructing* New Yorker *Cartoons, in* HOW ABOUT NEVER—IS NEVER GOOD FOR YOU? MY LIFE IN CARTOONS (New York: Henry Holt, 2014).

186 **"I guess I've stolen—I actually prefer the word 'borrowed'—as many ideas from Sol Price as from anybody else in the business"** Sam Walton & John Huey, SAM WALTON: MADE IN AMERICA 102 (Toronto: Bantam, 2012).

187 **"soccer is educational TV"** Mia Hamm & Aaron Heifetz, GO FOR THE GOAL: A CHAMPION'S GUIDE TO WINNING IN SOCCER AND LIFE 19–20 (New York: HarperCollins, 2000).

CHAPTER 10

196 **"We cannot think clearly about a plant or animal until we have a name for it"** Edward O. Wilson, THE FUTURE OF LIFE xvii (New York: Knopf, 2002).

196 **"the power of symbols and language"** Susanne K. Langer, PHILOSOPHY IN A NEW KEY: A STUDY IN THE SYMBOLISM OF REASON, RITE, AND ART (Cambridge: Harvard University Press, 1961).

196 **"the notion of giving something a name is the vastest generative idea that ever was conceived"** *Id.* at 142.

196 **"an MBA from Stanford"** Patt Morrison, *Patt Morrison Asks: Well Versed, Dana Gioia*, CHICAGO TRIBUNE (Nov. 5, 2011), *available at* http://www.chicagotribune.com/la-oe-morrison-dana-gioia-20111105-column.html ("I became the only person in history to go to Stanford Business School to become a poet.").

197 **"helping preserve America's rich artistic legacy"** *President Bush Presents National Medal of Arts, Awards Cultural Leaders*, NATIONAL ENDOWMENT FOR THE ARTS MAGAZINE, 2008, no. 5, at 15, *available at* https://www.arts.gov/NEARTS/2008v5-music-our-ears/president-bush-presents-national-medal-arts-awards-cultural-leaders.

197 **"productive tenure as head of the National Endowment of the Arts"** *Id.*

197 **"increased the understanding and appreciation of the arts among our nation's youth"** *Id.*

197 **"General Foods"** Nanette Byrnes, *The Man Who Saved the NEA: Businessman-Poet Dana Gioia Has Steered the Once-Moribund Arts Agency in Mostly Mainstream Directions and It's Thriving*, BLOOMBERG (Nov. 13, 2006), *available at* https://www.bloomberg.com/news/articles/2006-11-13/the-man-who-saved-the-neabusinessweek-business-news-stock-market-and-financial-advice.

197 **"Jell-O Jigglers"** *Id.*

197 **"First published"** Dana Gioia, *Words, in* INTERROGATIONS AT NOON 3 (Minneapolis: Graywolf Press, 2001).

197 **"The world does not need words"** *Id.*

198 **"no less real"** *Id.*

198 **"the dialect of pure being"** *Id.*

198 **"conjugal, covert"** *Id.*

199 **"arrowheads"** *Id.*

199 **"To name is to know and remember"** *Id.*

200 **"Skill and creativity are not necessarily innate"** *See generally* Berend Scholten, *Feyenoord Mourn Former Coach Wiel Coerver*, UEFA (Apr. 22, 2011), *available at* http://www.uefa.com/memberassociations/association=ned/news/newsid=1622631.html; *Dutch Soccer Guru Wiel Coerver Dies (86)*, RNW MEDIA, *available at* https://www.rnw.org/archive/dutch-soccer-guru-wiel-coerver-dies-86.

200   **"Coerver method"** Wiel Coerver, SOCCER FUNDAMENTALS FOR PLAYERS AND COACHES (Upper Saddle River: Prentice Hall, 2005); 1-2-3 GOAL TRAINING FOR EXCITING AND PRODUCTIVE SOCCER (2014) (directed by Wiel Coerver).

200   **"Axel Paulsen"** James Hines, FIGURE SKATING: A HISTORY 101–102 (Champaign: University of Illinois Press, 2006).

200   **"Johan Cruyff"** *See The Netherlands' Grand Master*, FIFA, *available at* https://bit.ly/2HYvWCp.

APPENDIX A

212   **"Stretch goal"** Sim B. Sitkin, C. Chet Miller & Kelly E. See, *The Stretch Goal Paradox*, HARVARD BUSINESS REVIEW, Jan.–Feb. 2017, at 92, *available at* https://hbr.org/2017/01/the-stretch-goal-paradox.

ACKNOWLEDGMENTS

You can't create a book on writing and editing without a lot of help from the writing and editing of other people. Among those who improved individual chapters are Ramzi Abboud, Julie Aust, Dave Babbe, Christina Cincilla, James Coatsworth, Dan Dalton, Shai Dothan, Samir Hanna, Hannah Hoffman, Akash Patel, Purvi Patel, Darien Perry, Scotti Peterson, Lydia Pincsak, Tim Pinto, Ben Preyss, Mansoor Quereshi, Stephen Rees, André Rouillard, Helen Ryan, Joel Richert, Kimiko Varner, and Sage Wen. This is in addition to the great work done by editors at journals and blogs that published earlier versions of chapters: *The Stanford Law Review* ("The Words Under the Words"), *The Journal of Legal Education* ("Infinite Power of Grammar"), *Legal Communication and Rhetoric* ("The Rule of Three"), *Scribes Journal of Legal Writing* ("Uselessly Accurate"), *Michigan Bar Journal* ("Good Sentences" and "Corresponding Ideas in Corresponding Forms"), and the *Appellate Advocacy Blog* ("The Power of the Particular" and "A Note About Passive Constructions").

I would also like to thank David Baum, Lisa Bernstein, Bridgette Carr, John Lemmer, Vivek Sankaran, and David Santacroce for offering crucial support even before any part of this book was drafted. Encouragement is an important form of advocacy.

On the production side of things, Jason Colman, Amanda Karby, and the rest of the folks at University of Michigan Publishing Services have showed me that when you have the right team, you can do some really helpful, innovative things in the world of books. I am already excited to get working on our follow-up project, *The Syntax of Sports*. Perhaps we'll even get to partner again with Scribe, the super-professional copyediting outfit that spearheaded the design of *Good with Words* and cleaned up the many errors that were in the manuscript I originally sent. (Whatever errors remain—and I imagine there are some—I am the only one to blame.)

Finally, and most especially, I'd like to thank the close to eighty students who took a chance on this course the first year it was offered at the University of Michigan Law School. We met for two hours every Friday afternoon, which I know is nobody's favorite time to work on syntax and semicolons. But each of them showed up, contributed to class discussion, and dramatically improved the way I think and write. I'm looking forward to tracking all of their very promising legal careers.